Copyright © 2023 Philip Careen

Disclaimer

The content in this book is provided for educational and informational purposes only. No responsibility can be taken for any result or outcomes resulting from the use of this material.

While every attempt has been made to provide information that is both accurate and effective, the author does not assume any responsibility for the accuracy or use/misuse of this information.

Table of Contents

CHAPTER ONE

CHAPTER ONE

INTRODUCTION

The Fundamentals of cheese production

Making cheese is the process of removing some milk constituents such as water, lactose, and minerals in order to produce a concentrate of milk fat and protein. Cheese is made from milk, coagulating enzyme (rennet), bacterial cultures, and salt. Rennet causes milk proteins to aggregate, transforming fluid milk into a semi-firm gel known as curd. When you cut this gel into cubes, the whey (mostly water and lactose) separates from the curds. Acid, a byproduct of bacterial activity, aids in the expulsion of whey from the curd and largely determines the moisture content, flavor, and texture of the cheese.

Milk

Milk is an essential liquid sustains life, it is made up of 4 components which are:

- Casein is the protein component of milk and such has structure which makes some cheese unique.
- Fat is the energy components of milk and it is responsible for milk flavor and aroma.
- Lactose is also an energy component also known as milk sugar which provides energy to microorganisms used in cheese production.
- Whey has the lowest percentage of whole milk, it is generally water combined minerals.

In cheese making, each of these components plays a vital role in the final curd formation.

Bacterial cultures (starter)

Starter culture is a mixture of un-harmful bacteria (lactobacilli, lactocci etc) that is added to milk to raise the acidity level. When the culture is added, it feeds on the lactose in the milk to produce lactic acid, which develops the flavor of the milk. There are two types of cheese cultures: mesophilic and thermophilic cultures Mesophilic cultures are moderate-temperature microscopic organisms utilized when the curds won't be warmed to higher than 102°F. Mesophilic cultures are commonly utilized for Cheddars, Goudas, and other hard cheeses. Thermophilic cultures are higher-temperature microscopic organisms that can live up to 132°F. They are used to make harder Italian cheeses like Parmesan and Romano as well as Swiss-style cheeses. These starter cultures play a crucial role in the flavor enhancement of the harder cheeses in addition to acidifying milk. Starter cultures are available in two forms:

1. Mother culture.
2. Direct set

How to make cheese mother culture

The cheese mother culture, which is made by reserving a small portion of the milk or whey from the previous day's work and storing it for the future, is a thick, yogurt-like mixture of milk and a combination of different strains of bacteria that are added to increase the acidity level of the milk.

Ingredients

- 4 cups skim milk
- Mother culture starter

Procedure

1. Ensure that you sterilize your tools in a pot of boiling water.
2. You can sterilize milk by heating it for 20 minutes over low heat in a container to kill bacteria that could otherwise kill some crucial bacteria.
3. After the milk has reached room temperature, inoculate it. Add your starter culture, close the container, and gently shake to maintain the temperature for at least 15

hours for mesophilic cultures and 6 hours for thermophilic cultures at 75°F or 110°F, respectively. You'll have a container full of substances that resemble yogurt when you're finished. Keep the mother culture in the refrigerator, but place it in the freezer for no more than three months if you don't intend to use it.

How to make direct-set culture

The only difference between direct-set cultures and mother cultures is that the bacteria strains are grown in a lab. This culture is simple for beginners because it is prepared and produces good results.

Rennet is necessary for making hard cheeses because it acts as a catalyst for the coagulation of milk and creates astronger curd. There are two types of rennet that are frequently used: animal type and vegetable type. Animal rennet is made from an enzyme called chymosin that is found in the stomach of unweaned herbivorous animals, whereas vegetable rennet is made from a mold called muror miehei that also contains an enzyme called chymosin. For home cheese makers, rennet and starter cultures are essential because they ensure consistent results. Animal rennet produces more solid curds than vegetable rennet, and when aged for a long time, vegetable rennet typically imparts a bitter flavor. To evenly distribute the rennet throughout the milk, make sure to dissolve the rennet in non-chlorinated water before adding it.

Calcium chloride This ingredient is crucial when making cheese, particularly when using milk that has undergone homogenization and high-temperature pasteurization or milk that has a low solids content (curds). Calcium chloride, which is frequently used in the production of goat cheese and some other hard cheeses, will improve milk coagulation when compared to using only rennet. 60ml of cool water should be added after adding 1ml of calcium chloride per gallon of milk.

The pH System The ph scale, which measures acidity or alkalinity on a scale from 0 to 14, is a tool used by cheese makers. At level 7, water and other neutral substances can be found. Levels 8 through 14 indicate alkalinity, while levels 6-0 indicate acidity, in that order. Milk has a pH of 6.6 while fresh cheeses have a pH of 4.5. Due to the additional lactic acid that fresh cheeses contain, which gives the cheese a pucker-like flavor.

External cheese and fungi Bacteria

Molds are fungi, aerobic organisms (they require oxygen), and they feed on foods with a lot of protein and moisture. The molds begin to grow on the surface of the cheese after being applied, and only then do they begin to penetrate the interior. At this stage, they will consume the milk's lactic acid to produce gases that have an ammonia-like odor. The process of softening fats and proteins with the help of this gas is regulated by factors like humidity, time, and temperature. A list of typical cheese molds for home use is provided below.

Name of mold	Description	Purpose
Geotrichum candidum	For a more appealing appearance, this ripening bacterium is frequently mixed with other bacterial species.	1. It promotes the growth of B linens 2. It prevents the cheese's rind from slipping off.
Penicillum candidum	This culture, which is whitish, works through the cheese as it ripens.	It gives cheese like brie an airy appearance.
Penicillium roqueforti	This surface bacteria causes cheese to ripen from the outside (surface) to the interior.	1. It's used to make blue cheese 2. It gives cheese a mushroom-like flavor.
Brev bacterium linens	This bacteria is a surface-ripening bacteria.	It gives cheeses a robust flavor note.

Salt

Salt is an essential ingredient that must be considered. Because salt prevents the growth of microscopic organisms, it is used at the end of the cheese-making process to slow the growth of lactic bacteria as well as to prevent the growth of any unidentified bacteria that may have gotten into the cheese. Additionally, salt acts as a dehydrator by drying out the cheese, which reduces the size of the curd structure. Salt gives cheese additional flavor. Use less essential table salt when making cheese because it frequently contains iodine. When making cheese, it's crucial to use non-iodized salt because iodine will impede or prevent the growth of the starter culture in the cheese. You can always use cheese salt or kosher salt among other types of salt.

Techniques for making cheese

It takes both art and science to make cheese. Home cheesemakers rely on pH readings and inoculations of particular molds just as much as they do on their own senses of sight, touch, and smell. When converting milk into cheese, there are six crucial steps they are:

<u>Acidification</u> Which is the first step in the cheese-making process. In this phase, milk is given a starter culture that will convert the milk sugar lactose into lactic acid. This starts the process of turning milk from a liquid into a solid and alters the amount of acidity in the milk.

<u>Coagulation</u> The process of converting a liquid into a semisolid is called coagulation. Rennet, an enzyme, is added when making cheese to help the milk coagulate.

<u>Whey and Curds</u> Milk coagulate into curd and whey as it cools. Whey is the liquid, and curds are the solid component. The curds are cut with a knife in this step. The curds are further encouraged to expel whey when they are cut. The smaller the curds are cut the harder the final cheese. Camembert and Brie are two common soft cheeses that are hardly ever cut. Cheddar and Gruyere are two examples of harder cheeses that can be grated very

finely. The curds are further worked by cheddaring and/or cooking for these harder cheeses. The curd's texture is altered during cooking, becoming tender as opposed to crumbly. The whey is removed after this procedure is done, leaving the curd alone to mature into cheese.

<u>Salting</u> For flavor, salt is added. Additionally, it serves as a preservative to prevent spoilage of the cheese during the protracted months or years that it is aged, and it aids in the formation of the cheese's natural rind. Salt can be used in a variety of ways. While making cheese, salt can be added directly into the curd. Salt or a damp cloth dipped in brine can be used to rub the outside of the cheese wheel (heavily salted water). As with mozzarella, the cheese can also be bathed directly in a brine vat.

<u>Shaping</u> Each type of cheese now assumes its recognizable shape as a solid block or wheel. To shape the cheese into a particular shape, it is placed into a mold or basket. In order to remove any remaining liquid, the cheese is also pressed simultaneously using weights or a machine.

<u>Ripening</u> This procedure, known as affinage, ages cheese to the ideal level of ripeness. The temperature and humidity of the cave or space where the cheese ages are closely watched during this period. Each cheese must be handled carefully by an experienced affineur in order for it to develop the desired flavor and texture. Some cheeses have a unique flavor because of ambient molds in the air. Others introduce mold by injecting it into the cheese or spraying it on the cheese (Brie) (blue cheese). Some cheeses require turning, oil brushing, or brine or alcohol washing before eating. The type of cheese and the cheesemaker's desired results determine how long a cheese is left to ripen. A cheese can age for several months to many years, but once it is done, it is ready for packaging.

Advice for a successful cheese maker at home

1. First, clean your equipment by sanitizing anything that will come into contact with the milk or curd before you start. By submerging your equipment in hot water. Additionally, remember to wash your hands.
2. Begin with easy cheeses. The majority of you have never made cheese before; if that describes you, try starting with easier cheeses before moving on to more difficult varieties.
3. Selecting milk. Making cheese with milk that has been pasteurized and homogenized in stores should be acceptable. Always read the label and steer clear of milk that has been "UHT," "ultra-pasteurized," or "micro-filtered." If you want higher-quality store-bought milk for making cheese, look for non-homogenized milk. Health food stores frequently carry this kind of milk. Today, 99.9% of cheese-making facilities use non-homogenized milk. And what about raw milk? Raw milk is milk in its unaltered, unheated, and un-homogenized natural state. It is being poured directly into a container from an animal, such as a cow, goat, sheep, water buffalo. Even though it must be handled carefully, this kind of milk is the best choice for making cheese.
4. Adding culture. It is advised to keep in mind the three SSS when adding culture. That is to SPREAD your culture over the top, allow it to SIT there for three minutes, and then gently stir. With this technique, your culture can easily and evenly dissolve into the milk and rehydrate on the milk's surface.
5. Adding rennet. It is advised to add rennet by allowing the rennet tablet (one-fourth of a tablet) to dissolve in one-fourth cup of non-chlorinated water 15 to 20 minutes beforehand. In order to be at its most potent before being added to the milk, the rennet enzyme needs time to "wake up" in water. To make sure that all of the grainy rennet mixture—rennet and water—is added to the milk and not left at the bottom of the measuring cup (1/4 cup), flush the measuring cup with milk after adding the mixture.
6. Non-chlorinated water, is water that has been distilled, bottled, or chlorinated tap water that has been heated to kill the chlorine and cooled to room temperature.
7. Use of your thermometer. For a more precise milk temperature reading, check the middle of the pot when checking the temperature of your milk with thermometer.
8. Clean break. Rennet will cause milk to change from a liquid to a semi-solid state. A knife mark will remain on a well-formed curd. Look for a cut line in your curd after you stab it with a knife. Your curd is too weak if your knife mark vanishes. Give it some more time to sit. Testing for a "clean break" is another, more sophisticated

method to determine when your curd is ready. This is accomplished by gently lifting/levering your finger or knife upward after gently inserting it into the curd at a 45-degree angle. Your curd should then "break cleanly" into a clearly defined line.

9. Stirring method. A "top-down stirring" technique is used in cheese making. Pulling the milk from the top down to the bottom and back up to the top again is the method used for stirring. A gentle up-and-down motion that aids in evenly distributing your ingredients throughout the milk. You should avoid stirring in a circular or whirlpool motion.

10. Improve as you go all skilled cheese makers gain knowledge with each batch.

Ingredients and Equipment for Making Cheese

Since making cheese is an artistic and skilled process, having the right tools and equipment gives each cheese maker an advantage. The beauty of making cheese lies in the tools available to the maker. The following are the essential tools and equipment that every home cheese maker should possess:

1. Colander: You can use any type of colander, but I prefer one with a high footed base so the whey won't come into contact with the cheese.
2. Opened Spoon: This is a very fundamental tool for making cheese; I suggest stainless steel varieties.
3. A double boiler is a piece of kitchen equipment used to gently heat milk while making cheese.
4. Huge kitchen Pot: It is best to use a stainless steel pot because pure metallic pots, like aluminum pots, can react with the acid present and contaminate the cheese, making their consumption dangerous.
5. Cheese Cloth or Butter Muslin: Since store-bought cheese cloth has a free weave, it is suitable only for fresh cheeses. Its quick accessibility and extreme modesty are advantages. The alternative is butter muslin. As long as you wash it in your sterilizing solution after use, it has a much tighter weave, is more grounded, and is reusable. The main drawback of butter muslin is that it can only be purchased online or at cheese supply shops, which puts you in a difficult situation if you decide to make cheese right away. You'll find that by doubling the cheese cloth, the results for the basic cheeses in this book turn out to be quite good. However, it is preferable to take the necessary steps and obtain the butter muslin when you enter the more advanced stages of cheese making. Avoid confusing yourself by throwing away some cheese that could be fantastic because of a piece of cheese cloth.
6. Thermometer: You'll need a dairy thermometer. You can use an instant-read thermometer or one that will attach to the side of the pot for continuous monitoring. An electronic, thermometer is a great choice if you want to try something new because it has an alarm for precise settings. Having two thermometers running at once when using a double boiler will give you better control over the temperature of your milk.
7. Cheese Press: When making hard cheeses, a cheese press is a necessary tool. When cheese is placed inside of a perforated mold, a cheese press exerts pressure on the cheese. The watery whey drains out and is thrown away as the pressure is raised, and the cheese wheel solidifies and assumes its final shape.

8. Cheese Follower: They cheese press is topped with a thin, flat piece of plastic called a cheese follower. The follower moves downward in the mold when pressure is applied because its diameter is just a little bit smaller than that of the mold. A follower produces an even cheese by evenly dispersing the press's weight over the cheese's surface.

9. Curd knife: You simply need a long knife that can reach the bottom of the pot. The ideal blade should be thin and capable of making precise cuts.

10. Cheese Board: Once your cheese has been removed from the cheese press, you will need a cheese board to dry it. Before each use, sterilize the board in a steam bath for twenty minutes. Use a wooden board instead of plastic because plastic won't let any cheese moisture through.

11. Cheese Molds: The mold determines the shape of the cheese. Molds are plastic shapes with holes in them that are used to hold curd while it drains. There are many different sizes and shapes of cheese molds, and many of them have unique shapes that have historically been associated with particular kinds of cheese.

12. A cheese trier is a necessary tool when making any hard cheese. Without having to cut it open, a slice of cheese can be tested using the trier. You simply core out a sample to check if the cheese is done mostly from the center. The small amount that was lost will be made up for by the cheese.

13. Mini Fan: This extra tool will evenly distribute humidity and prevent the growth of mold in the refrigerator. Close the door on the cord, place it away from the cheese, and plug it into an outlet.

Advance cheese making techniques

Cutting cheese

Before cutting the curds after coagulation, you must check that they have the proper consistency, which happens when the rennet has completed its task. More whey will be released when the curds are cut, a process known as syneresis (contraction of the curd leads to the release of more whey). The whey from the curds must also be removed after **renneting** because it contains lactic acid that could make the curds too acidic to produce cheese. To do this, use the stirring and scalding curds method. Curds are stirred to keep them in suspension because, if they are not stirred, they will clump together in large masses and prevent the release of whey.

<u>Scalding</u> involves raising the temperature of the cut curds; as the temperature rises, the rate at which the whey drains also rises.

<u>Colored cheese</u>: Some cheeses, like Colby and cheddar, have a characteristically yellow color that does not come from the milk. One common food coloring used in cheese is annatto seed, which is a native of Central America.

<u>Milling</u> They process of milling involves breaking the drained curds into tiny pieces with your hands. Note that the size of the curds does affect the cheese's texture; smaller curds will produce a hard cheese, while larger cuds will produce a soft, smooth cheese.

<u>Salting</u> There are two popular ways to salt chess:

1. Dry salting, which involves simply combining salt with drained curds by sprinkling salt over the curds and mixing with clean hands. If the salt is properly combined, it will dehydrate the curds, causing them to shrink and allow the curds to bind together in the mold.

2. Brine-salting: In this method, the cheese is immersed in a supersaturated salt solution (brine), which is made by combining 2 cups of salt with 1 teaspoon of calcium chloride and white vinegar in 16 cups of water heated to 150°F. As the cheese absorbs the salt, the protein at the surface begins to set and form a ring.

<u>Pressing</u> The final whey is released from the curds during pressing, which is a necessary step in the production of hard cheese. Under-pressed cheese is typically dense because this whey wasn't released, while over-pressed cheese will have the whey released.

<u>Turning</u> The cheese must be turned by being flipped over end to end in order to avoid being uneven and having a rough texture. You must do it once per week for ripened cheese.

<u>Catch pan</u> Delicate aged cheeses have a high moisture content, so they will drain a lot of whey. The best method for this is to use a catch pan, typically an 8" x 8" baking dish.

<u>Drying mat</u> A drying mat is essential for making mold-aged cheeses because it provides a permeable barrier that prevents the cheese from accumulating moisture on its base.Two drying mats that have been disinfected in boiling water for 20 minutes are needed. Sushi mats made of bamboo or plastic work well as drying mats.

<u>Cheese film</u> a breathable cellophane wrap called "cheese film" will add a protective barrier to your cheese and allow the shape to develop.

<u>Waxing, natural ring, or cloth banding</u>

There are three ways to protect the surface of aged cheese: cloth banding, natural rings, and waxing. Aged cheese typically requires that its surface be protected. Cheeses are typically preserved by cloth banding, which involves wrapping a cloth bandage tightly around the cheese to promote the development of a rind.

Banding the Cheese Method

• Lay a perfect sheet of cheese cloth over the cheese, trace the top and bottom of the cheese, and cut out four circles that are each large enough to cover the cheese's sides. Spread a thin layer of vegetable shortening over the entire piece of cheese. Sticking to the shortening, place the cheese cloth on the cheese's top and base.

• Repeat the process, with an additional layer of shortening between the two layers of fabric. Apply the second layer of cheese cloth on top, smoothing the surface to create a tight seal. Ripen for 3-6 months at 55°F with 80-85 percent humidity, turning every week.

When cheese is left to ripen in a room for a prolonged period of time, a natural rind develops. The exterior of the cheese naturally loses moisture, which causes its crust to harden and become dense. It is best to clean the cheese with brine solution while natural rings are forming.

Waxing is a method used to keep cheese from drying out and to stop mold from growing on the cheese's exterior. Despite being porous, wax does not permit a complete exchange of moisture the way a cloth band does. On the other hand, waxing might be the best option if you prefer cheese that is softer and more moist, and it is a simple process. The lifespan of the various cheeses is increased by a wax coating that helps cheese retain moisture while preventing mold.

Note: Using a different type of pot could be stressful; waxing is simply done in a stainless-stccl stockpot.

A Brief History of Cheese Production

The word cheese is derived from Latin caseus, Cheese is an old food with origins dating back before recorded history. Its origins and history are frequently reflected in the way of life, individuals, innovation, and legislative issues of the era in which it arose. Simply put, cheese reflects who we are, our taste preferences and the types of milk available. Cheesemaking has been traced back to roughly 8000 BCE, when sheep were first domesticated. Since animal skins and inflated internal organs have been used as storage vessels for a variety of foodstuffs since ancient times, it is likely that the process of cheese making was discovered accidentally by storing milk in a container made from an animal's stomach, resulting in the milk being turned to curd and whey by the rennet from the stomach. The earliest archaeological evidence of cheesemaking goes back to 5500 BCE and is found in what is now Kuyavia, Poland, where strainers coated with milk-fat molecules have been discovered. The hundreds of years old techniques for making cheese have influenced how modern cheese looks and tastes, and the techniques have changed little for the specialist. The Romans were known in ancient times for their love of cheese because it was so important to their diet that they carried it everywhere. The Roman Empire is frequently credited with profoundly influencing the creation and utilization of cheese as it spread its ideas and innovation throughout its conquered lands.

The modern era

Until the modern spread of European culture, cheese was virtually unknown in east Asian cultures and the pre-Columbian Americas, and had only limited use in sub-Mediterranean Africa, being most common and popular in Europe, the Middle East, the Indian subcontinent, and areas influenced by those cultures. However, as European imperialism and, later, Euro-American culture and gastronomy spread, cheese gradually became known and increasingly popular globally. Although the first facility for industrial cheese production started in Switzerland in 1815, large-scale manufacture found genuine success in the United States. Jesse Williams, a dairy farmer from Rome, is usually credited with pioneering the assembly-line production of cheese utilizing milk from surrounding farms in 1851. Hundreds of similar dairy associations existed within a few decades. The first mass-produced rennet appeared in the 1860s, and by the turn of the century, scientists were manufacturing pure microbial cultures. Previously, bacteria in cheese production had come from the environment or through reusing an earlier batch's whey; the pure cultures allowed for more uniform cheese production. In the World War II era, factory-made cheese surpassed traditional cheesemaking, and factories have been the primary supplier of cheese in America and Europe ever since. Cheese was one of the top shoplifted commodities from supermarkets worldwide by 2012. In the 21st century people have developed a taste for small artisan cheeses that have always been a part of Europe as a result of globalization.

Why make your own cheeses

Making cheese at home may appear to be a task for professionals. In any case, with such a diverse selection of cheese recipes in this book, getting started is simple, and there are numerous reasons to make your own cheese at home.

o   The best ingredients are used to make homemade cheese.

Artificial colors and additives may be included in commercial cheeses. Making your own cheese allows you to select your own ingredients and determine what works best for you.

o   It's extremely simple

There are a few basic steps to making cheese, and they are all the same regardless of the type of cheese you want to make. Once you've mastered those steps, you can make any cheese you want. You don't need much equipments to make cheese, which makes it very simple.

o   It's comes out delicious

Your handcrafted cheese will be edible regardless of the type of cheese you make. The most amazing and unusual cheeses were discovered unintentionally. Regardless of whether you believe you've completely ruined your cheese, drain, salt, and try again. You may never have the opportunity to repeat it, but you can still enjoy eating it.

o   It's a hit among kids.

Children enjoy making cheese. Children enjoy eating cheese. Cheese-making is a fun culinary pastime for youngsters. They can take part and learn as they go. Cheesemaking is a unique approach to educate science and chemistry if you home school.

o   It is a rare skill.

Simply put, there aren't that many people who know how to do it anymore. A handcrafted cheese is always a hit. Do you want to become a specialist? Begin with simple cultures like Cream Cheese Starter Culture and progress to hard cheeses like Cheddar or Colby made with Mesophilic Starter Culture. The best ingredients are used in custom-made cheese. Inorganic colorants or added substances may be found in commercial cheeses. Making cheese at home allows you to use whatever ingredients you want and what works best for you.

Cheese consumption and health

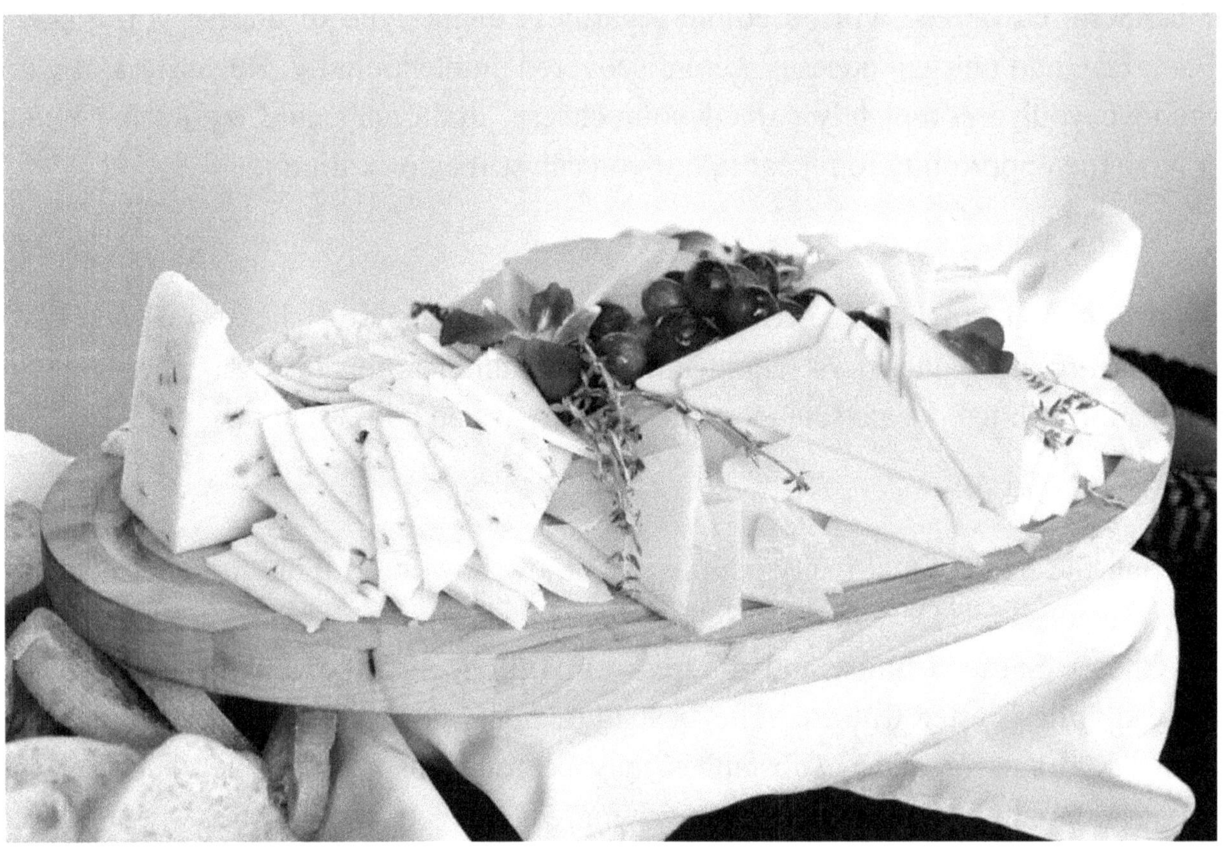

Cheese is a high-nutrient dairy product that contains protein, lipids, and minerals (calcium, phosphorous, Vitamins A, B12). Cheese may be tolerated better than milk by certain people because it contains less lactose, a form of sugar that is difficult to stomach if people lack the enzyme to break it down. Cheese contains a variety of nutrients. One ounce of hard cheese, or a wedge, has around 120 calories, 8 grams of protein, 6 grams of saturated fat, and 180 milligrams (mg) of calcium. A half-cup of soft cheese, such as full-fat cottage cheese, contains around 120 calories, 14 grams of protein, 3 grams of saturated fat, and 80 milligrams of calcium. Most cheeses are heavy in sodium, with 300-450 mg per serving, because salt is an important element in retaining moisture and preventing bacterial overgrowth. Some cheeses, such as goat, whole-milk mozzarella, and Swiss, are low in salt, containing only 50-100 mg per serving. Full-fat dairy products are high in saturated fat and include some cholesterol. Milk fat contains around 70% saturated fat, 25% monounsaturated fat, and 5% polyunsaturated fat. Because a high saturated fat diet can raise LDL cholesterol levels, which affect the heart, it is generally advised to lower the rate of cheese consumption. Also consuming limited amount of cheese can lower the risk of cardiovascular diseases due to the specific nutrients like calcium and mono-polyunsaturated fats. The truth is that cheese is considered a full food. Whole foods are generally healthy, as long as you don't eat too much of one thing at a time. Below are the reasons why you should incorporate cheese to your diet.

- Cheese has the ability to prevent osteoporosis.

Osteoporosis is a bone disease that causes the bone to become fragile and porous; it is the leading cause of fracture. Osteoporosis is caused primarily by poor calcium absorption or consumption, as it is well known that milk contains calcium on its own. This is why parents instruct their children to drink milk on a regular basis due to its high calcium and vitamin D content. To prevent this disease, it is best to consume dairy products, with cheese being the best option.

- Cheese can improve your dental health

Because cheese contains calcium and vitamin D, which are responsible for strong bone and teeth, eating it can help with tooth growth and development.

- Cheese is an Excellent Protein Source

Protein is a basic nutrient that is responsible for the growth and repair of worn out tissues. A lack of protein causes a slew of health issues, which is why protein is such an important food nutrient. The body does not store excess protein, which is why your daily food intake should include protein, and because cheese is an excellent source of protein (it contains essential amino acids), eating it on a daily basis poses no risk.

- Cheese is rich in vitamin B12.

Vitamin B-12 (also known as Cobalamin) is the largest and most complex vitamin found today. It promotes the production of red blood cells, protein, and DNA, as well as numerous psychological health benefits. Vitamin B-12 deficiency illness is the result of an insufficiency, which can cause fatigue, muscle weakness, and neurological damage. This basic vitamin is normally found in animals and is required in the body for vital functions; cheese is a rich source of cobalamin, so eating cheese on a daily basis will deposit a significant amount of vitamin B12

- An essential fat, is found in cheese

Conjugated linoleic acid is a complex compound produced by grass-fed animals that plays an important role in the immune and inflammatory systems, aids in bone formation, and lowers the risk of heart attacks.

- Cheese May Aid in the Prevention of Certain Cancers

Cheese contains vitamin D, calcium, and lactic acid, which protects the body system from some cancerous growth in some body systems and can help prevent one of the most common cancers that affect the digestive and colon systems (cancer of the colon).

- Cheese is an Excellent Pregnancy Food

Pregnant women require calcium for a variety of metabolic reasons, including preeclampsia, a condition in which a pregnant woman develops hypertension during pregnancy, which can harm the fetus. Would you prefer to buy synthetic calcium that might have adverse effect or eat calcium rich food like cheese, doctors usually recommend cheese for pregnant women.

- Cheese is high in the essential vitamin K2.

The vitamin K2 is notable for its role in assisting blood clotting; it acts as a co-factor that stimulates enzyme activities. This vitamin interacts with a variety of vitamins and supplements, including calcium and vitamin D. It benefits your bone, skin, and dental health by transporting and retaining these essential nutrients and minerals in these areas. It can help prevent dementia in the elderly by encouraging healthy brain activities.

- Cheese is Beneficial to Thyroid Health

Your thyroid, a small, butterfly-shaped organ in your neck, is probably not something you think about very often, but it should if you're concerned about your health. The hormones it produces regulate nearly all of the body's metabolic activities; excessive (hyperthyroidism) or insufficient (hypothyroidism) production of these hormones can throw your body off balance. Thyroid disorders can cause a wide range of side effects. These include (hypothyroidism), weight gain, and weakness. Why for (hyperthyroidism) infertility, anxiety, insomnia, and rapid weight loss which may lead to more serious problems in the future. There are numerous things you can do to avoid developing a thyroid disorder, and one of the most practical is through nutrition. Consuming iodine and selenium helps to prevent thyroid disorder, and these two elements are abundant in many cheeses, particularly hard cheeses.

- It has a lot of nutrients.

Cheese is high in calcium, fat, and protein. It is also high in vitamins A, B12, and D, as well as zinc, phosphorus, and riboflavin. The overall nutritional profile of conventional, organic, and grass-fed dairy products is identical, according to US Dairy. Grass-fed cheese is created from the milk of cows that have only been fed grass. A diet strong in grass-fed dairy may provide a more balanced diet. Trusted source of omega-6 and omega-3 fatty acids than traditional dairy diets. Omega-3 fatty acids are essential for heart and metabolic function.

Cheese classification

Cheeses are categorized into three types:

Lactic Acid/Rennin Based Cheese: These types of cheese are classified according to whether the curd is created by the activity of lactic acid or by the action of the rennet (rennin) enzyme, and they are further classified as follows:

Acid-curd cheese or Cottage cheese: To make this cheese, either the milk is left to sour naturally or Streptococcus lactis or lactobacilli are inoculated to grow in it until they create enough acid to allow the milk to curdle. The curd is removed from the whey, salted, and shaped into balls or cakes. The cheese is now ready to be eaten. Such cheese cannot be stored for lengthy periods of time because moulds and yeasts begin to grow, destroying the flavor and other characteristics of the cheese making it bad for consumption.

Cheese made using rennet: The action of the rennet (rennin) enzyme results in a wide range of cheeses. Rennet-curd cheese is further classified into two types: Soft rennet-curd cheese and hard rennet-curd cheese

Soft Rennet-curd Cheese (50% to 80% water): These cheeses have poor aging characteristics and a short ripening period. Those produced by bacterial action are known as Limburger and Liederkranz and their variants; those produced by mould action are known as Camembert and Brie.

<u>Rennet-curd Hard Cheese (less than 40% water)</u>: Hard rennet-curd cheese has a long ripening period, generally with good looking qualities, and can be stored for years. Cheddar and Swiss cheeses are examples of hard rennet-curd cheeses in which bacteria play an important role in the curing process. Roquefort and Lowa blue cheese are examples of hard rennet-curd cheeses where the ripening process is primarily carried out by moulds.

<u>Cheese based on fat content</u>: Cheese Can Be Divided into Two Types Based on Fat Content: high-fat cheese and low-fat cheese.

1. High-fat Cheese: Curd with additional cream to increase fat content to 60% or higher.
2. Low-fat Cheese: Curd made without additional cream, with a fat content of less than 60%.

<u>Cheese Based on Physical State of Structure</u>: The cheese can be easily classified into three categories based on its physical state of structure, they are:

- Soft Cheese: This category of cheese includes ripened and unripened varieties, they are listed below:
1. Un-ripened cheese (Cottage, Gorgenzola, Stilton)
2. Bacteria-ripened cheese (Limburger),
3. Mould-ripened cheese (Camembert cheese, Brie cheese).

- Semi-hard Cheese: This category only includes ripened cheese that is neither soft nor hard. Bacteria and molds work together to ripen the cheese. Semi-hard cheese is classified into the following types and subtypes:
1. Mould-ripened cheese (such as Gorgonzola, Roquefort, and Stilton)
2. Bacteria-ripened cheese (Brick cheese, Muenster cheese).

- Hard Cheese: These are ripened cheeses with a hard texture. All of the hard cheeses are only bacteria-ripened. The following hard cheese types and subtypes are available:
1. Cheese with gas holes (Swiss and Parmesan)
2. Cheese without gas holes (Cheddar and Edam).

CHAPTER TWO

CLASSIC CHEESE RECIPES

German quark cheese

Prep time: 5 minutes

Cook time: 2 minutes

Rest time: 1 day

Total time: 1 day 7 minutes

Yield: 1 pound

Ingredients

- 1 gallon milk
- 2 tablespoons buttermilk
- Salt (optional)

Procedures:

1. Warm the milk to 88°F, stir in the starter culture (buttermilk).
2. Cover the milk and let it age at room temperature for 24 hours, or on the other hand until the milk has set (it ought to have the consistency of a firm yogurt).
3. After the mixture sets, empty it into a colander lined with cheese cloth and tie it into a ball, let it be suspended from a wooden spoon.
4. Allow the cheese drain in your refrigerator all night, with a catch bowl put below the colander. Once the whey has emptied, remove it from the colander and the cheese cloth, place it in an airtight refrigerator container, and store in the refrigerator for as long as about fourteen days.

Paneer

Prep Time: 2 hrs 30 minutes

Cook Time: 15 minutes

Total Time: 2 hrs 45 minutes

Ingredients:

- 8 cups whole milk
- 6 tablespoons lemon juice or diluted white vinegar
- A pinch of salt

Instructions:

1. Over medium heat, pour the milk into a large pot and bring it to a boil. Take the milk off the stove. Remove the froth or skin by skimming it.
2. As the curds begin to separate, gradually add the lemon or vinegar water while stirring very slowly and gently. Excessive or vigorous stirring will break them up and result in smaller curds, which is not what you want.
3. The milk may begin to curdle after you stir in the acidic medium. For the curds to fully separate, cover the milk and let it sit for 10 minutes.
4. After that, remove the pot and get ready to drain. Place a colander into a mixing bowl after lining it with cheesecloth.
5. Carefully transfer the curds to the colander from the pot (lined with cheesecloth). Drip the whey into the bowl below.
6. When the majority of the whey has been strained, add salt to the cheesecloth and gently stir. To remove the vinegar or lemon juice from the curds, rinse them under cold water. Additionally, this aids in cooling the milk curds so that you can squeeze it right away.
7. The cheesecloth should be gathered into its four corners and tied together, either by hanging it from a wood spoon placed over a large bowl.
8. Place the cheese on a kitchen towel after carefully unwrapping it. Split the curds. Using the heel of your hand, squeeze the towel to help it absorb more liquid. Add salt, then gently mix it in.
9. Create a disc out of the cheese (wrapped). To press the cheese that has been wrapped for two hours, place 10 pounds on top. Before using the cheese in a recipe, chill it.

Nutrition

Calories: 605kcal

Carbohydrates: 49.8g	Protein: 30.9g	Fat: 32g	Fiber: 0.1g	Cholesterol: 97mg

Chèvre cheese

Prep time: 5 minutes

Rest time: 12 hours

Cook time: 5 minutes

Total time: 12 hours 10 minutes

Yield: ½ pound

Ingredients:

- ½ gallon whole goat's milk
- ½ packet chevre culture
- ½ drop of rennet dissolved in 1 tablespoons of water
- 1 teaspoon Calcium chloride diluted in 28ml of water (for pasteurized milk)
- Salt to taste (optional)

Method:

1. Heat the milk in a pot over medium heat until it reaches 86 °F.
2. Sprinkle the chevre culture over the milk's surface and let it hydrate for two minutes before stirring it in.
3. Mix for 60 seconds after adding diluted rennet.
4. Cheese curds will form before the 12-hour period has passed if the milk is covered; if not, extend the resting period by an additional 5 hours.
5. When the curds are neatly cut and completely separated, place them in a cheese cloth-lined colander with a catch bowl below.
6. To ensure that the whey is properly drained, roll the cheesecloth into a ball and fold the closures over a wooden spoon.
7. The cheese is ready when the whey stops draining, usually between four and six hours. Take the cheese out of the cloth, season it with salt, and then place it in a tight container. Keep cold until you're ready to eat.

Farmers cheese tvorog

Prep time: 2 minutes

Rest time: 1 minute

Cook time: 5 minutes

Total time: 8 minutes

Ingredients

- 1 gallon whole milk
- ½ cup white vinegar

Procedure

1. Do not boil the milk; instead, heat it over medium-low heat until hundreds of tiny bubbles begin to appear. To keep the milk from burning at the bottom of the pot, stir it occasionally.
2. Add a half cup of distilled white vinegar gradually, stir it gently, and wait for 60 seconds. Re-stir then. The water should be a light lime/yellow color, and the cheese will curdle (become crumbly). If not, add a little more vinegar until the water does turn that color. Take off the heat and allow to cool to room temperature.
3. Line a colander with a cheese cloth. Slowly pour the cheese into the cloth to catch the curds. Gather the cloth around cheese and squeeze it as much as you can to get all the whey out. When you start seeing white-ish liquid coming out instead of lime color, you can stop there.
4. Refrigerate cheese and store for up to a week.

Yogurt

Prep time: 5 minutes

Rest time: 12 hours

Cook time: 5 minutes

Total time: 12 hours 10 minutes

Yield: 1gallon

Ingredients:

- ½ gallon milk
- ¾ pack of yogurt starter
- Salt (optional)

Procedure:

1. Heat the milk in a pan until it reaches 180° F, about 5 minutes. The more time you keep the milk at this temperature, the more concentrated it becomes. Take the milk off the heat, then let it cool to 110°F.
2. Dissolve the starter culture in a small amount of milk in a cup. Pour this mixture into the milk pan and stir to evenly distribute the yogurt culture.
3. When the mixture reaches the desired consistency, incubate it for at least 4 hours while keeping the milk covered and heated to 120°F. To ensure a strong culture, let the yogurt sit at room temperature for an additional 6–12 hours after it has set.
4. Place the finished yogurt in an airtight container and store in the fridge for up to 14 days. To make Greek yogurt, strain it.

Reminder: Save the whey from Greek cheese for baking or making ricotta cheese.

Nutrition per serving

Calories: 124

Carbohydrates 12g	Protein 8g	Fat 5g	Cholesterol 14mg

Yogurt Cheese

Prep time: 5 minutes

Rest time: 24 hours

Yield: 2 cups

Ingredients:

2 pounds yogurt

Procedure:

1. Place a colander on a catch bowl and line it with two layers of cheesecloth.
2. Pour the yogurt into the lined colander, cover it with the cheesecloth, and let the whey drain without pressing.
3. The yogurt, colander, and catch bowl should all be placed in the refrigerator to drain for 6 to 12 hours. The colander should be covered with plastic wrap or a clean towel. Keep the whey; it is healthy and useful in a variety of recipes.
4. Roll the cheesecloth into a ball, then wrap a wooden spoon in the closures. Place the wooden spoon on the container's edges to suspend the yogurt over a bowl or stock pot, leaving space for the whey to drain into the container.
5. Until the cheese reaches the desired consistency, let the pile of cheese drain in the refrigerator for an additional 8 to 12 hours without touching it.
6. Scrape the cheese into a storage container, and use it within two weeks.

Cream Cheese

Prep time: 5 minutes

Cook time: 10 minutes

Rest time: 5 hours

Total time: 5 hours 15 minutes

Yield: ½ pound

Ingredients:

- 1 cup whole milk
- 1 cup half and half
- 2 cups heavy cream
- ¼ cup lemon juice
- ½ teaspoon salt

Instructions:

1. If you intend to use the whey later, line a colander with large cheesecloth and place it over a big bowl. Make sure your cheese cloth extends well past the colander edges.
2. Heat a pot with the milk, salt and creams on medium heat. Heat for about 5 minutes, to a temperature between 165 and 170 °F.
3. Add the lemon juice and continue stirring for a couple of minutes. The milk/cream will start to simmer a little bit and a light foam will start to form, along with the formation of curds that rise to the top. Soft curds will begin to form, but they won't be as firm as mozzarella curds; rather, they'll be much softer and more like clouds.
4. Once you notice them forming, turn off the heat, let it sit for an additional minute, and then take it off the heat.
5. After 2 minutes, gently scoop some curds into the cheesecloth with a large spoon, and then slowly and carefully pour the remaining curds and whey into the cheesecloth. Note: The curds frequently appear to be very soft and cloud-like and may be difficult to scoop. If so, simply pour the liquid into the cheesecloth and let it drain.
6. Cheesecloth can be simply drained in a sieve or colander lined with cheesecloth, or the edges can be gathered and suspended over a kitchen faucet. You can gently squeeze the cheesecloth that has been wrapped around the object to let some whey out, let drain for 1-4 hours.

7. Turn cheese into a sizable bowl after carefully opening the cheese cloth. If it still seems a little loose, don't worry; it will thicken a little more as it chills in the refrigerator.
8. It will thicken if the bowl is covered with plastic wrap or placed inside of an airtight container and allowed to cool for at least three hours. Store for up to two months in the freezer or for about a week in the refrigerator.

Nutrition

Calories: 177kcal

Carbohydrates: 3g	Protein: 2g	Fat: 18g	Fiber: 1g	Cholesterol: 64mg

Cottage cheese

Prep time: 5 minutes

Cook time: 5 minutes

Rest time: 1 hour

Total time: 1 hour 10 minutes

Yield: ½ pound

Ingredients:

- 2 cups whole milk
- 3 tablespoons vinegar
- 1 cup heavy cream

Instruction:

1. Over medium heat, while stirring occasionally, warm the milk to 180°F.
2. Remove milk from heat when it reaches 180°F, then stir in vinegar right away. Curds will begin to form.
3. Give the curds and whey at least 30 minutes to reach room temperature.
4. Cheesecloth folded twice is used to line a colander. Place the colander in a large bowl or the sink. The lined colander should now contain the curds and whey. Allow to drain for five minutes. (The whey can be thrown away or saved and added to another recipe.)
5. To gather the curds into a tight ball, gather the cheesecloth's edges together. Squeeze the ball gently over the sink with clean hands to let more whey out.
6. Run the ball under gently running water and squeeze it again if you're worried about a vinegar taste lingering.
7. With a fork, gently mash the curds of the cheese ball in a bowl. Add the heavy cream and stir. You'll discover that the cream is easily absorbed by the curds, leaving little liquid in the finished cottage cheese. Your cheese is set

Ricotta

Prep time: 5 minutes

Cook time: 25 minutes

Rest time: 5 days

Total time: 5 days 30 minutes

Ingredients:

- 4 cups pasteurized milk or whey
- 1 tablespoon lemon juice
- 2 tablespoons vinegar
- ½ tablespoons Salt

Instructions:

1. Set a colander in the sink with three layers of cheesecloth inside. Lemon juice and vinegar should be combined in a measuring cup.
2. Heat the milk and salt to 185°F in a Dutch oven or large saucepan over medium-high heat. To avoid scorching, stir frequently with a rubber spatula.
3. After removing the pot from the heat, gently stir in the lemon mixture for about 15 seconds, or until the mixture curdles.
4. Allow to stand for 10 minutes without stirring, or until the mixture completely separates into opaque whey and solid curds.
5. If the whey still appears milky and the curds haven't completely separated, add 1 tablespoon of vinegar and continue to sit for 2 to 3 minutes. Continue doing this until the curds separate.
6. Pour the curds into the prepared colander gently. Allow to stand still about 8 minutes or until whey has drained from the cheese's edges but the center is still very moist.
7. Transfer the cheese carefully to a large bowl while preserving as much of the whey inside the cheese as you can. To break up large curds and incorporate whey, stir thoroughly.
8. Place in the refrigerator for up to 5 days or until very cold. Before using, stir the ricotta.

Nutrition per Serving: Calories: 73kcal

Carbohydrates: 6g	Protein: 4g	Fat: 4g	Fiber: 1g	Cholesterol: 12mg

Gjetost and Myseost

Prep time: 5 minutes

Cook time: 2 minutes

Rest time: 30 minutes

Total time: 37 minutes

Ingredients:

- 1 gallon fresh whey
- 1 cup heavy cream

Procedures:

1. Pour all of the whey into a large pot. To avoid it bubbling over, leave plenty of room at the top. Add the cream, gradually raise the temperature until it boils. When the mixture begins to bubble, reduce the heat to a simmer and skim the froth that has formed on the pot's surface, don't discard the froth.
2. Place it in a bowl and store it in the fridge. Boil the whey while occasionally stirring to prevent it from sticking to the pan's bottom.

3. Add the saved froth and mix when the whey has reduced to about 80% of its original volume. Continue to boil, stirring to keep the cheese smooth, to reduce even more.
4. Pour the mixture into a pan when it resembles fudge and place it in a water bath to cool. To remove any chunks, continue mixing in the container.
5. Put it in an airtight container and refrigerate to set it once it has started to solidify. Refrigerate at a temperature of about 40 °F and 90% humidity. For three weeks, gjetost and myseost will stay fresh in the refrigerator and should be firm enough to cut.

Serac cheese

Ingredient

Fresh whey

Procedures

1. Heat the Whey to 185°F after straining it through butter muslin. Allow to rest for 20 minutes.
2. After 20 minutes, place the curds that have floated to the top into tiny cheese molds. In the molds, the cheese ought to drain and cool.

Cotswold

Prep time: 10 minutes

Cook time: 60 minutes

Rest time: 4 hours

Total time: 5 hours 10 minutes

Ingredients:

- 1 Gallon of Milk (Not Ultra Pasteurized)
- 1 teaspoon Blanched Garlic Scapes or Chives
- 1 tablespoon Dried Onion Bits
- ½ Packets C101 Mesophilic Culture
- ¼ teaspoon Single Strength Liquid Rennet
- Cheese Salt
- ½ teaspoon Calcium Chloride (for pasteurized milk)
- Herbs (optional)

Instructions:

1. With about ¼ cup of boiling water, rehydrate the onion for 30 seconds, then filter the bits and set it aside.
2. To blanch garlic, simply place it in boiling water for 45 minutes, remove it, and then immediately submerge it in cold water to kill any unwanted bacteria.
3. Refrigerate the combined onion and garlic until you're ready to combine them with the drained curds for pressing.
4. The milk should first be heated to 90°F. To accomplish this, put the milk in a pot with very warm water. Make sure to heat the milk slowly and stir it well as it heats.
5. Add about ½ teaspoon of calcium chloride to the milk if it is pasteurized.
6. The culture can be added once the milk reaches 90°F. Sprinkle the powder over the milk's surface to prevent it from caking and sinking in clumps. Next, wait about 2 minutes for the powder to rehydrate before stirring it in.
7. Until it is time to raise the temperature to cook the curds, the milk must now be kept at this target temperature. Hold the milk that has had culture added gently for the next 60 minutes to enable the culture to start working. After that, add a quarter of a teaspoon of liquid rennet.

8. The milk must now rest quietly for 60 minutes while the rennet coagulates the curd and the culture works. Let the milk rest for another 60 minutes for a good curd formation, even though you'll notice the milk starting to thicken around 20 minutes.
9. Ensure that your molds, cloth, colander, and other materials are clean and prepared. Next, determine if the curd has set. When the curd breaks, you want to look for a neat split in the curd. Wait a few more minutes for a firmer curd and add a little more rennet if it still seems soft.
10. When the curd passes the testing, it is time to cut it for whey separation.
11. Start by making a large cross hatch cut that is ¾ to 1 inch vertical only. Wait about 5 minutes for this to firm up before moving on to the final cut for this cheese, which is about 3/8 inch and will shrink to ¼ inch when it has finished cooking.
12. After the cut is complete, give the curds a few minutes to settle before giving them a 10-minute very gentle stir. The curd should have further solidified by this point and be ready for cooking, which will further dry them out.
13. It's time to start drying the curds now. The heat will be gradually increased to 102°F to accomplish this. At first, the heat must be gradually increased by about 5°F every five minutes.
14. If the curds are still soft after an additional 15 minutes of cooking, the total cooking time will be increased to 60 minutes.
15. The final curds should be thoroughly cooked before being checked to see if enough moisture has been drawn out. When pressed between the fingers, a broken curd should resist pressure only slightly. It should be firm throughout.
16. The curds can now be allowed to settle beneath the whey once this point is reached. Then take away the whey that was above the curds.
17. The curds can then be poured into a butter muslin-lined colander. A gentle stir of the curds will ensure that the whey drains off after the recommended 30 minutes of draining.
18. After that, add salt and wait for the curds to absurd the salt for 5 minutes. The herbs can be added and stirred in after the salt has been added.
19. The draining cloth can now be folded over the curds before placing them in the prepared molds. Press and after that, the cheese can be waxed.

Pepper Jack

Prep time: 10 minutes

Cook time: 60 minutes

Rest time: 3 hours 30 minutes

Total time: 4 hours 40 minutes

Serving: 1 pound

Ingredients:

- 1 Gallon of Milk (Not Ultra-pasteurized)
- ½ Packet C101 Mesophilic Culture
- ¼ teaspoon Single Strength Liquid Rennet
- Salt
- 1 teaspoon smoked jalapenos
- 1 teaspoon peppercorns
- ½ teaspoon Calcium Chloride (for pasteurized milk)

Instructions:

1. The milk should first be heated to 88 °F. To accomplish this, put the milk in a pot or sink filled with very warm water. Make sure to heat the milk slowly and stir it thoroughly as it warms up if you're doing this in a pot on the stove.
2. The culture can be added once the milk reaches 88°F. Sprinkle the powder over the milk's surface to prevent it from caking and sinking in clumps. Next, wait about 2 minutes for the powder to rehydrate before stirring it in.
3. After thoroughly incorporating the culture, let the milk sit for 60 minutes as the culture gets to work.
4. To bring out the oils and flavors in peppercorns, briefly toast them in a pan over medium heat until they pop. Then use a mortar and pestle to slightly crack them.
5. Stir in rennet into the milk. The milk must now rest quietly for 45 minutes while the rennet coagulates the curd and the culture works. It's important to keep in mind that the curd starts to thicken at around 15 minutes, but it needs the full 20 minutes to be firm enough for a cheese like this.
6. This milk should remain warm during this time due to its thermal mass. If the temperature falls a few degrees during this time, it's okay.

7. The whey that rises should not be too cloudy or too clear, and the edges of the curd should show clean breaks when it is finished.

8. It is time to begin the solids and liquids separation once you have a good break. For this cheese, I usually start by making vertical cuts in a checkerboard pattern between 1/2 and 5/8 inches. I next rested this for three to five minutes, or until the whey started to rise and flood the surface. When you make the horizontal cut into curds, this will firm up the freshly cut surfaces and make them more difficult to break.

9. Next, make horizontal cuts with your spoon. When finished, the curds should be about ½ inches

10. When finished then, start a slow, gentle stir from the bottom to the top to keep the curds moving and separated. Let these settle and rest for an additional 3 to 5 inches to firm up as in the first cut. Keep in mind that they are currently very fragile.

11. If the temperature has dropped at all, bring it back up to 88°F as the curds continue to move in the warm whey. For about 10 minutes, stir in a gentle manner.

12. It's time to start drying the curds. Over the next 30 minutes, gradually raising the temperature to 95°F will accomplish this. At first, the heat must be gradually increased by 3°F every five minutes.

13. After that, cook for an additional 30 to 60 minutes.

14. If the curds are still soft, use the longer time; otherwise, the total heating and cooking time will be 60–90 minutes.

15. The final curds should be thoroughly cooked before being checked to see if enough moisture has been drawn out. When pressed between the fingers, a broken curd should resist pressure only slightly. It should be firm throughout. The curds can then be allowed to settle beneath the whey once this point is reached.

16. After that, discard the whey and replace it with cool water. This will result in cheese that is sweeter and more moist. Start by taking out roughly 40 percent of the whey, leaving about an inch of whey covering the curds.

17. After that, start immediately washing the curds in cold water. Once the curd stabilizes at a temperature of about 75°F, slowly add cool water while stirring for about 15 minutes. Since the temperature has dropped to the low end of the culture's operating range, it will also serve to slow the bacteria.

18. Now that the curds are dry, they can be moved to a colander where they should be gently stirred and allowed to drain for a few minutes. Mix the hot pepper into the cheese after adding it. As soon as the curds have thoroughly drained, add salt while they are still in the draining colander. Salt should be added in two or three doses and stirred in until the curd absorbed it.

19. The cheese cloth should now be pulled up, smoothed, and then folded as close to the surface as you can. Make sure the surface is as smooth as you can. The cheese is currently ready for press. The press weight should be very light to start, and then gradually increase to a moderate level.
20. Give the cheese surface some time to dry; it might take a few days. The cheese surface can be waxed for aging once it has dried.

Mascarpone

Prep time: 3 minutes

Cook time: 3 minutes

Rest time: 4 hours

Total time: 10 minutes

Ingredients:

- 2 cups whipping cream
- 1 tablespoon lemon juice

Procedure:

1. When the cream reaches 185°F, add the lemon juice and stir for 3 minutes over a low heat. Take it off the heat and let it cool.

2. Pour the mixture into a colander lined with cheesecloth and place it over a catch bowl. Place the cheese and its catch bowl in the refrigerator after covering it with the cheese cloth's closures.
3. Drain the cheese until it reaches the desired consistency about 1-4 hours. Once the cheese has drained, take it out of the cheese cloth and place it in a container to chill for up to a month.

Nutrition

Calories: 108 kcal

Carbohydrates 1g	Protein 1g	Fat 12g	Fiber 1g	Cholesterol 43mg

Cantal cheese

Prep time: 5 minutes

Cook time: 5 minutes

Rest time: 12 hours

Total time: 12 hours, 10 minutes

Yield: 2 pounds

Ingredients:

- 1 gallon whole milk
- 4 tablespoons mesophilic mother culture, or ¼ teaspoon direct-set culture
- ¼ teaspoon calcium chloride
- ¾ teaspoon liquid animal rennet
- 2 teaspoons cheese salt

Instruction:

1. Once the milk has reached 90°F, carefully stir in the starter culture before covering. Give the milk 45 minutes to ripen. If you're using homogenized milk, add calcium chloride.
2. Rennet should be added while the milk is still at 90°F, and the mixture should be gentle. Use a curd blade to cut through the curds and check for a total separation after 60 minutes of covering and setting. Cut the curds into ¼ " (6 mm) pieces. Stir for 30 minutes and let the mixture settle to the bottom.
3. Place a colander on your drain bowl, line it with cheese cloth or butter muslin, and pour the curds into the colander.
4. Drain for 20 minutes, making sure that there is enough whey left over to keep the curds moist.
5. Once more, add the salt to the cooking pot with the curds. Mix well with your hands. To maintain the desired temperature, let the pot rest in the water bath for ten minutes.
6. Curds should be placed in a cheesecloth-lined mold. Given that the curd still contains whey, get your catch bowl ready. Cheese cloth should be placed over one edge of the curds before pressing at 20 pounds for 30 minutes.

7. Remove the cheese from the press, covering it with cheese cloth, and allowing it to rest for eight hours at room temperature on a cheese board. This step is unique to Cantal and is thought to be where the lactic acid develops, giving the cheese its remarkably rich flavor.

8. Cut the curds into ¼ " pieces. Put the curds back in the mold and press them for two hours at 40 pounds. Rewrap the cheese with the cheese cloth after removing it from the mold and cheese cloth. For a full day, press at fifty pounds.

9. Unwrap the cheese after removing it from the mold. For a few days, let the cheese air-dry on a wooden board while turning it frequently. The cheese is ready for ripening when it feels dry to the touch. For 3-5 months, let cheese ripen in a refrigerator at 45°-55°F and 80–85% humidity.

10. Every day, flip the cheese over and wash it with a salt solution made from 1 tablespoon of salt dissolved in 2 cups of water. The cheese is set for use.

Halloumi

Prep time: 5 minutes

Cook time: 50 minutes

Rest time: 2 hours

Total time: 2 hours, 55 minutes

Yield: 2 pounds

Ingredients:

- 1 gallon goat milk or whole milk
- 4 tablespoons mesophilic mother culture, or ¼ teaspoon mesophilic direct-set culture
- ¼ teaspoon calcium chloride
- ½ teaspoon fluid rennet
- ½ cup cheese salt for brine solution
- 1 teaspoon dried mint, rehydrated in ½ cup boiling water

Procedures:

1. In a double boiler, heat the milk to 86°F. Add the starter culture at this point, and stir for two minutes. Maintaining an objective temperature of 86°F, add the rennet, stir briefly to ensure proper distribution, and let rest for 60 minutes, or until complete separation.
2. Make sure to maintain as much uniformity as you can when cutting the curds into ½ " (or 1 cm) cubes.
3. After 10 minutes of resting, gradually heat curds to 104 degrees Fahrenheit; this should take 45 minutes.
4. To prevent the curds from tangling, consistently stir them. When the curds reach the desired temperature, stir them continuously for an additional 30 minutes.
5. Whey from curds should be drained into a cheesecloth-lined colander that is placed in a catch bowl. If needed, keep the whey in storage.
6. The curds should be drained before adding the mint. Fill a 2-pound cheesecloth-lined mold with the curds. Place a cheese cloth edge over the curds, press for 60 minutes at 30 pounds.
7. Cut the cheese after removing it from the mold. Reverse the cheese and cover it once more with cheesecloth. For 60 minutes, press at 40 pounds.
8. In a dish, heat the preserved whey to 190°F. Cut the cheese into 2" (5 cm) thick strips after removing it from the mold.
9. Place the strips in the warmed whey and hold them there for 60 minutes at the desired temperature. The cheese should be thick in texture. Drain it into the colander lined with cheese cloth, and then let it sit at room temperature for 20 minutes.
10. Take the cheese slices out, sprinkle a little salt on each side, and then place them on a cooling rack to air dry for a while.
11. Halloumi pieces are placed in a brine made of 50% leftover whey, 20% boiling water, and 10% salt. The cheese can be kept in the brine for up to two weeks in the refrigerator.

Pyrenees

Prep time: 2 minutes

Cook time: 20 minutes

Rest time: 1 hour

Total time: 1 hour, 22 minutes

Ingredients:

- 1 gallon whole milk
- ¼ teaspoon fluid rennet dissolved
- ¼ teaspoon calcium chloride
- 4 tablespoons mesophilic mother culture, or ¼ teaspoon mesophilic direct-set culture
- 1 tablespoon cheese salt

Instruction:

1. Add the starter culture to the 90°F warm milk, stir, and maintain the desired temperature for 45 minutes. Calcium chloride should be added after stirring for a minute.
2. Gently stir in the rennet. For 45 minutes, cover and place in a secure location. You'll notice that the curd has hardened. When looking for a complete break or separation, use your finger or a blade.
3. Cut the curds into ½ " (or 1 cm) cubes. Place the pot in a heated water bath, and for about 30 minutes, gradually raise the temperature until 100°F is reached. As the curds continue to shrink, you'll notice that more whey will rise to the top.
4. Once the desired temperature has been reached, cover for five more minutes before draining the curds into a colander over a catch bowl that is lined with cheesecloth or butter muslin.
5. Put the curds in a ball and hang them for 60 minutes to drain from a wooden spoon that is resting on the edge of a stock pot. At first, you'll notice a lot of whey draining from the curds. The ball will be solid, soggy, and ready for use after 60 minutes.

Feta

Prep time: 5 minutes

Cook time: 10 minutes

Rest time: 12 hours

Total time: 12 hours, 15 minutes

Ingredients:

- ½ cup plain low-fat yogurt with live cultures
- 1 gallon whole milk (pasteurized)
- ¼ teaspoon lipase powder preferably calf
- ¾ teaspoon calcium chloride
- ¼ teaspoon liquid rennet vegetable or animal
- 3 tablespoons kosher salt

- Reserved Whey

Instructions:

1. Combine the yogurt and ½ cup of the milk in a small bowl.
2. The remaining milk should be heated in a deep pot over medium-low heat for 10-12 minutes, occasionally stirring with a slotted spoon until it reaches 90°F. Add the yogurt mixture and stir. Leave the pot on the burner after turning the heat off, cover it, and let it sit for 45 minutes.
3. Spoon. Give it 20 minutes to sit. Once the mixture is smooth and well-combined, add the calcium chloride and rennet and stir.
4. The milk mixture should be heated to 98°F over a medium-low heat before adding the lipase mixture and stirring for a minute.
5. After removing the pot from the heat, leave it covered and unattended for 1-3 hours, or until the curd is firm and has a clean "break."
6. Use a table knife to crosshatch the curd in an inch-long pattern from the top of the pot to the bottom. Put the heat on low for five minutes. At 98°F, stir the curd with a slotted spoon.
7. After removing the pot from the heat, cover it, and let it sit for a full hour while stirring it to break up any large chunks.
8. Over a large bowl, place a large colander that is lined with two layers of cheesecloth.
9. Put the curd in a strainer and let it sit there for 30 minutes to drain the whey. Four cups of the whey should be saved, covered, and left at room temperature.
10. Cheesecloth ends should be gathered, tied loosely at the top of the curd, and then tied around a long spoon. While loosely covering the top of the pot with plastic wrap, hang the cloth inside for 8-12 hours (overnight is best) at room temperature. If not, let the curd hang for a few more hours and check again; you should then feel a firm, solid mass of curds.
11. Transfer the feta to a cutting board after releasing the cheesecloth's tie. Feta should be divided into 2-3-inch pieces.
12. Place the squares in a sterile shallow container with a tight-fitting lid. Arrange them in a single layer. For the next one to three days, or until the cheese is firm, sprinkle 1 tablespoon of salt evenly over the cheese, cover it, and place it in the refrigerator. As the whey gathers in the bottom of the container, pour it off.
13. Clean up a big lidded container. Place the cheese pieces in the container; you may now arrange them however you like. The 2 tablespoons of kosher salt should be dissolved after being stirred into the reserved whey. Place the cheese in the

refrigerator for one to four weeks after pouring this brine over it. The flavor and texture of aged feta will become more intense as it ages. The cheese is ready.

Beaufort cheese

Prep time: 5 minutes

Cook time: 60 minutes

Rest time: 70 minutes

Total time: 2 hours 15 minutes

Serves: ½ pound

Ingredients:

- 2 Gallons whole milk
- ¼ teaspoon MA011 Culture or 1 Packets C101 Mesophilic Culture
- 3/8 tsp TA061 Culture
- 1/16 teaspoon LH100 Culture
- ¼ tsp Single Strength Liquid Rennet
- Brine solution
- Calcium Chloride (for pasteurized milk)

Procedures:

1. To 90°F, warm the whole milk. After adding cultures and letting them ripen at 90°F for 30 minutes, add ¼ teaspoon of liquid rennet diluted in ¼ cup cool, non-chlorinated water, and let it sit for 35 minutes.

2. After the curd has rested for about 5 minutes, cut it vertically into a ¾ to 1 inch matrix or grid. Next, cut the curd into cubes measuring ¼ inch. The whey will rise in the cuts as the curd rests for an additional 5 minutes.
3. For 60 minutes, gradually heat the curds to 128-130°F. While cooking, gently stir the curds to prevent them from matting. To the level of the curd, drain the whey.
4. Using cheesecloth, line the mold. Place the lined molds inside of a container. Move the curds and remaining whey into the cheese mold after pouring the drained whey into it.
5. Press with 30-pound weight for 30 minutes. The curd can be made to evenly consolidate and eliminate small holes by pressing under the whey.
6. After draining the whey from the mold and re-molding the curds, flip them over. Then press for 120 minutes with 30 pounds of weight, then gradually increase the weight to 100 pounds and press for an additional 7 hours at 85°F to allow the acid to further develop.
7. Remove the cheese from the mold and turn it over after each weight increase. After pressing is complete, remove the weight and cheese mold and let the mixture rest for a day.
8. For 12 hours, submerge the cheese in a brine solution. Since the cheese will float, sprinkle a small amount of salt on top before turning it over and salting the other side. Repeat this process throughout the brining period.
9. Dry off the cheese's brine solution, then store it in a curing room or refrigerator at a temperature of 53 to 55 °F. After a week, mold will start to form, so you'll need to brush the mold with brine solution to remove it. Make sure to flip the cheese over after each round so that a red rind can form. Then age 6–12 months depending on the desired flavor.

Caerphilly cheese

Prep time: 5 minutes

Cook time: 30 minutes

Rest time: 3 hours

Total time: 3 hours 35 minutes

Serves: 2 pounds

Ingredients:

- 1 gallon whole milk
- 4 tablespoons mesophilic mother culture, or ¼ teaspoon mesophilic direct-set culture
- ¼ teaspoon calcium chloride diluted in ¼ cup cool water
- ½ teaspoon fluid rennet diluted in ¼ cup cool water
- 2 tablespoons cheese salt

Procedure:

1. In a double boiler, heat milk to 90°F. Add the starter culture and stir well. At the desired room temperature, cover and allow to rest for 30 minutes.
2. Add the rennet to the milk, mix for two minutes, and then cover while maintaining a temperature of 90°F.
3. Wait 60 minutes at the desired temperature, or until there is complete separation, before handling the mixture. Check for a clean cut after making one cut with a curd blade. Cut the curds into cubes that are 1/4" inch size, maintain a uniform size.
4. Bring the temperature up to 92°F gradually; this should take 10 minutes. Hold the curds for 40 minutes at the desired temperature.
5. Make sure to mix frequently to keep the curds from tangling and let them rest for five minutes at the desired temperature.
6. The whey should drain into a catch bowl after the curds have been drained into a colander lined with cheesecloth. Slice the curds into 1-inch-thick pieces, then stack them on top of one another. In a short period of time, turn the stack several times from top to bottom.
7. Break the curds into thumbnail-sized pieces with your hands, then combine with salt. The salted curds should be put into a 2-pound mold lined with cheese cloth. Press the curds at ten pounds for 10 minutes while covering them with one corner of the cheese cloth.
8. Open the cheese cloth, take the cheese out of the press, and take it out of the mold. Before rewrapping with cheese cloth, turn the cheese over and sprinkle salt over the top and bottom of the block. Ten minutes of 20-pound pressing. Use a similar technique again, pressing for 20 minutes at 25 pounds. Use a similar approach again, pressing for 16 hours at 25 pounds.
9. After removing the cheese from the mold, let it dry naturally. It ought to take a few days. To ensure even drying, turn the cheese several times each day. When the cheddar feels dry to the touch, it is ready to be aged.
10. For three weeks, let cheese ripen in your refrigerator at 55 degrees Fahrenheit and 80 to 85 percent humidity.

Cheddar cheese

Prep time: 10 minutes

Cook time: 50 minutes

Rest time: 5 hours

Total time: 6 hours

Ingredients:

- 2 gallons cow or goat milk
- 1/8 teaspoon. calcium chloride diluted in ¼ cup water (optional)
- 1 packet direct-set mesophilic culture
- ½ teaspoon liquid animal rennet dissolved in ½ cup cool water
- 2 tablespoons sea salt

Instructions:

1. Warm the milk to 85°F in a big pot by stirring it frequently. Add the calcium chloride (if needed), as the milk is heating. Add the culture when the milk reaches 85°F, stir it in, cover and let sit for an hour.
2. After homogenizing the milk, slowly stir in the diluted rennet.
3. Take the cheese off the heat and let it sit for an hour, or until the whey starts to separate from the curd, before serving. The curd should be floating on top of a layer of mostly clear whey and pulling away from the sides of the pot.
4. Cut the curds into 1/4-inch cubes with a kitchen knife, then set aside for 5 minutes to set. Keep still.
5. Stirring frequently, slowly bring the curds' temperature to 100°F over the next 30 minutes. The curds will shrink as you stir. Maintain the temperature and keep stirring for the following 30 minutes after the curds reach 100°F. Remove from heat if the curds become too hot. Stop stirring after 30 minutes and let the curds sink to the bottom of the pot. About 20 minutes will pass during this.
6. Transfer the cheese to cheese cloth lined colander. Place the filled colander in the cheese pot, and let drain for 15 minutes.
7. Turn the curds out onto a cutting board after taking the colander out of the pot. You should have a jelly-like, semi-solid mass. Pour the whey back into the pot after cutting the mass into five slices. Cover.
8. Place the pot with the curds inside a sink that has been filled with 102°F water. For the following two hours, turn the slices every 15 minutes while maintaining the curds' temperature at about 100°F. This process is known as Cheddaring which is responsible for the distinct flavor and deliciousness of cheddar.
9. The curds will be shiny and very firm after two hours. Slice them into 1-inch cubes after removing them from the pot.
10. Put everything back in the pot, cover it, and put it in a sink with 102°F water.
11. Stir gently with your fingers or a wooden spoon after 10 minutes. Repeat two more times. Add salt after removing the pot from the sink and give one more gentle stir.
12. Put a piece of cheesecloth inside the cheese press and then carefully add the curds. For 15 minutes, press the cheese with the cloth wrapped around it at 10 pounds of pressure.
13. Unwrap, flip, and take the cheese out of the press. Rewrap using brand-new cheesecloth, then press for 12 hours at 40 pounds of pressure.
14. Unwrap, flip, and take the cheese out of the press. Rewrap using brand-new cheesecloth, then press for 24 hours at 50 pounds of pressure.
15. When the cheese is smooth and dry to the touch, remove it from the press and let it air dry for two-three days.

16. Wax the cheese and let it age for at least 60 days at 55 to 60 °F. Your cheddar cheese is done.

Cheshire cheese

Prep time: 5 minutes

Cook time: 10 minutes

Rest time: 2 hours

Total time: 2 hours 15 minutes

Serving: 2 pounds

Ingredients

- 2 Gallon of Milk (Not UltraPasteurized)
- ½ Packet C101 Mesophilic Culture
- 1 teaspoon Single Strength Liquid Rennet
- 1-2 teaspoon Annatto Cheese Coloring
- 2 tablespoons Cheese Salt

Instructions:

1. Heat milk to 88°F, higher temperature is good for milk with more fat. The culture can be added once the milk reaches the desired temperature.
2. Before stirring the powder into the milk, sprinkle it over the top and give it about 2 minutes to rehydrate. Mix well and allow to ripen for 60 minutes.

3. The color can be added after the culture has been thoroughly incorporated. The Annatto tree was used to make this extract. About 2 teaspoons of the color should be added to the milk for a Cheshire that is fully colored. It is best to first combine this with a small amount of milk before adding it to the entire batch. Before adding rennet, make sure the color has been stirred in for 10 to 15 minutes.

4. After giving the milk an hour to rest, stir in some diluted rennet. Let the milk coagulate using the rennet for one hour.

5. Once you discover a separation cut the curd into pieces between 1/2 and 3/4 inches wide, it can be stirred briefly before being left to sit for five minutes. For the next 60 minutes, stir infrequently as the mixture slowly heats to 88–90°F. The lactose slowly becomes acidified over the course of the following 30 minutes as the curd is allowed to pitch (settle to the bottom of the vat) and limit moisture loss.

6. Pour the curds into a colander that has been lined with cheese cloth or butter muslin to separate the whey. To help the curds consolidate for 15 minutes, the curd mass is wrapped in the draining cloth and weighted with 8–12 pounds. After that, it is cut into large cubes measuring 3 to 4 inches and turned over every 10 minutes (5 times). While it continues to drain, it is kept warm.

7. Continue doing this for another two hours, allowing the whey to freely drain from the broken curd pieces as the acid continues to develop. To improve whey drainage, open the cloth and flip the curds several times.

8. To slow the growth of bacteria and flush out the remaining whey, the curd can now be cut into 1/2- to 3/4-inch pieces and salted.

9. Once the salt has been absorbed, the cheese is transferred to a cloth-lined mold and put back into the pot in a water bath that is 80°F-hot to keep it warm.

10. The cheese is taken out of the mold the following morning, rewrapped in cloth, and put in a press. It will be gently pressed for about two days, rotating every day. In a 6 inch diameter mold, the weight starts out low at 12 to 20 pounds and rises gradually until it reaches 150 pounds. Unwrap, flip, and then rewrap the cheese after each change in press weight.

11. After being taken out of the press, the cheese is dried and waxed. It can be cured for as little as three weeks on shelves in a curing room at a temperature of 55 to 60°F, but the longer the curing period, the better the cheese.

Colby cheese

Prep time: 5 minutes

Cook time: 5 minutes

Rest time: 1 hour

Total time: 1 hour 10 minutes

Ingredients

- 2 gallons whole milk (raw or pasteurized)
- 1 packet direct-set mesophilic starter
- ½ teaspoon single strength rennet (dissolved in ¼ cup cool water)
- 2 Tablespoons cheese salt

Instructions:

1. The milk should first be heated to 86 °F. Add the starter culture, stir for about a minute to fully mix it in, and then let the milk sit for an hour to ripen.
2. Make sure the cheese is still around 86 degrees after an hour has passed. For one minute, add the diluted rennet and stir it up and down into the cheese. Stirring should be done for a few more minutes for raw farm fresh milk.
3. For 30 minutes, until the cheese has a clean break, cover the cheese and leave it alone.
4. Slice the curd into 3/8-inch pieces, give it a gentle stir, and then allow it to sit for five minutes.
5. By raising the whey's temperature 2 degrees every 5 minutes, you can bring the curds' temperature up to 102 °F. It's crucial to heat the curds gradually, and doing so by putting the pot in a sink full of hot water can help.
6. Keep the curds and whey at that temperature for 30 minutes after they reach 102. To prevent the curds from matting, stir occasionally.
7. Until the whey is at the same level as the curds, pour off the majority of it. Add cool 60 °F water while stirring until the water/whey reaches 80 °F. For 15 minutes, maintain a constant temperature of 80 ° while stirring frequently. (This extra water step, known as "washing the curds," aids in determining the cheese's final moisture content. A warmer mixture results in cheese that is dryer, whereas a cooler mixture results in cheese that is more moist.)
8. The curds should be poured into a cheesecloth-lined colander and left to drain for 20 minutes. The cheese salt should be gently incorporated into the sliced curds.

9. Put the salted curds in a cheese press that is lined with cheesecloth. For 20 minutes, apply pressure of 20 pounds.

10. Peel the cheesecloth off after removing the cheese from the mold. The cheese should be wrapped, turned over, and then put back into the press for 20 minutes at 30 pounds of pressure.

11. After removing the cheese, re-wrap it again, and flipping it, press it at 40 pounds for an hour. Repeat the flipping and re-wrap, then press for 12 hours at 50 pounds.

12. Remove the cheesecloth and the cheese from the press. The cheese must air dry for a number of days before it is dry on all sides. During this open drying, the cheese will be turned frequently.

13. Age the cheese for 60 to 90 days at 50 °F after waxing.

Gorgonzola Picante

Prep time: 5 minutes

Cook time: 5 minutes

Rest time: 2 hours 30 minutes

Total time: 2 hours 40 minutes

Servings: 1 pound

Ingredients:

- 2 Gallons of Milk (Not Ultra Pasteurized)
- 8 tablespoons Prepared Bulgarian Yogurt
- 1/16 teaspoon Penicillium Roqueforti
- ¼ teaspoon Liquid Single Strength Animal Rennet
- Salt

- ¼ teaspoon Calcium Chloride (for Pasteurized Milk)

Instructions:

1. Before beginning, mix 1/2 cup of milk with 1/16 to 1/8 teaspoon of blue mold powder and let it rehydrate for several hours.
2. Heat the milk to 87°F, stir it thoroughly. Stir in 6 tablespoons prepared bulgarian yogurt. Add milk that has had blue mold rehydrated. Allow to ripen for 30 minutes.
3. For a firm set, add ½ rennet and let sit for 60–90 minutes.
4. Cut curd into cubes measuring ½ to 3", then rest for 5 minutes before stirring for 1 hour.
5. Remove whey until it reaches the curd level, then put curds in a cheesecloth and let them drain overnight. Allow acid to develop at 68°F for a pH of 4.6–4.8 at the end.
6. Heat an additional gallon of whole milk to 87F the next morning. Add remaining prepared bulgarian yogurt, and then wait 30 minutes for it to ripen.
7. Add the remaining rennet, and then wait 90 minutes. Curd should be cut into ½ to ¾" pieces and stirred for a few hours after resting for five minutes. PH should be 5.9 after removing whey to curd level. Cut the first day's drained curds into pieces about the size of walnuts.
8. In a cheese mold lined with cheese cloth add fresh curds to the bottom, top with old cheese curds and then fill the mold with fresh curds to the edges. Press with 30 pounds weight.

9. To set the surfaces, remove cheese from mold, flip the curds, re-wrap and press every 30 minutes. Repeat this process until the next day.
10. Over the next five days, this cheese receives a lot of salt, with one day between applications. The distribution of the salting doses is 50%, 30%, and 20%.
11. The surface of the cheese will initially be rough and hard after dry salting, but after a few days the surface will become somewhat sticky and moist due to the salt absorbing into the cheese.
12. The cheese's texture will change, becoming softer, and the blue color will start to show on the surface around days 10–18. It's time to make holes in the cheese's exterior so that air can get to the blue interior.
13. Punch the top side of the cheese with a sterile needle or nail on day 15 and the bottom side on day 20.
14. Keep an eye out for the formation of a red rind. High moisture levels and a shift in surface pH are to blame for this. This needs to be removed
15. Ripen the cheese at 52–56°F and 92–97%. Avoid letting the rind get too sticky.
16. The cheese will be ready to eat after a nice slow aging in the cave for about 3-6 months.

Gouda

Prep time: 10 minutes

Cook time: 1 hour

Rest time: 3 hours

Total time: 4 hours 10 minutes

Ingredients:

- 1 Gallon whole Milk
- 4 ounce Mesophilic Starter Culture
- ½ teaspoon single strength rennet (dissolved in ¼ cup cool water)

Instructions:

1. The milk should be heated to 85 °F.
2. Mix well with a whisk after adding 4 oz of mesophilic starter culture; the culture must be evenly distributed throughout the milk. Add the rennet to the milk gradually while whisking the mixture constantly for at least five minutes.
3. Till a firm curd has formed and a clean break can be made, then cut the curds and let the curds sit for 2 hours.
4. Cut the curds into 1/2 inch cubes with a long knife. Ten minutes should be given for the curds to firm up.
5. Bring the milk's temperature up to 102 °F gradually about 45 minutes.
6. To prevent the curds from mating together during this time, gently stir them every 5 minutes.
7. Allow the curds to cool to 102 degrees before carefully scooping 3 cups of whey off the top.
8. Add three cups of 102 °F water to replace the lost whey.
9. The curds must cook for an additional 45 minutes at 102 °F. 3 cups of whey should be removed and replaced every 15 minutes with 102 °F water.
10. At the end of the procedure, whey will have been eliminated three times.
11. Pour the whey through a colander lined with cheesecloth to drain it.Put your cheesecloth-lined mold with the drained curds inside it with care.
12. For 45 minutes, press the cheese at a weight of about 20 pounds. Flip the cheese over after removing it from the press. For three hours, press the cheese at about 40 pounds.

13. As the cheese is still very soft, carefully remove it from the press and place it in a container with brine solution for three hours, let the cheese float in a cold brine solution. To ensure even rind development turn the cheese over every 45 minutes or so. When you pat the cheese dry, you'll see that the exterior has started to become harder.
14. Put the cheese in the refrigerator for 25 days to age. The cheese must be turned over each day to prevent uneven drying.
15. Keep turning the cheese every day and avoid covering it with plastic, however place the cheese in a covered container if an excessively thick rind starts to form.
16. Every day, check for mold. If mold does appear on the surface of the cheese, it can be easily removed with a paper towel dipped in white vinegar. After 25 days, you have the option of using it right away or further aging it by waxing.
17. Continue to flip the cheese every three days or so if you waxed it. Enjoy

Crottin de Chavignol

Prep time: 5 minutes

Cook time: 5 minutes

Rest time: 22 hours

Total time: 22 hours 10 minutes

Yield: 1 pound

Ingredients:

- 1Gallon of Goats Milk
- 1Packet C20G Chevre Culture
- 1/16 teaspoon C70 Geotrichum Candidum

- Cheese Salt
- Calcium Chloride (for pasteurized milk)

Instructions:

1. Milk should be warmed to 74 degrees before adding culture and letting the mixture sit for 2 minutes to allow the powder to rehydrate.
2. Combine milk with geotrichum mold allow to rest for 20 hours at target temperature.
3. The curd is ready to ladle once it has been separated from the container's sides with the whey on top.
4. In order to pre-drain the curd, line a colander with butter muslin. The curds can now be transferred with a ladle and left to drain in cheesecloth lined colander for 15 hours at 72°F.
5. The curds can be hung in the cloth to aid in draining after being collected and briefly drained. About halfway through the drainage, the cloth can be opened, and the curd mass can be lightly mixed to encourage even drainage.
6. The pre-drained curd is now set to be transferred to the Crottin molds at this point.
7. Fill the mold with curds as time goes on their mass will reduce by half in 12 hours.
8. Add a quarter teaspoon of cheese salt to the top of each curd in its mold about two hours after filling the molds.
9. The cheese can be taken out and put back into the mold the following morning. Each curd should have an additional ¼ teaspoon of cheese salt sprinkled on top.
10. The cheese should be taken out of the molds, placed on a dry surface, dried for two days, and aged for a minimum of two weeks.

Note: To age cheese, you need a high enough moisture level, so keep the cheese in the refrigerator and remember to gently rub the mold down to avoid thick rings.

Edam cheese

Prep time: 5 minutes

Cook time: 10 minutes

Rest time: 1 hour

Total time: 1 hour 15 minutes

Yield: 2 pounds

Ingredients:

- 2 gallons low-fat milk
- ¼ teaspoon MM 100 culture or ¼ teaspoon mesophilic direct-set culture
- ½ teaspoon calcium chloride diluted in ¼ cup cool water (pasteurized milk)

- 1 teaspoon fluid rennet
- Brine

Instruction:

1. Once the milk has reached 90°F, slowly stir in the starter culture before covering. Give the milk 20 minutes to age. If you're using homogenized milk, combine it with the diluted calcium chloride.
2. As long as the temperature is kept at 90°F, add the diluted rennet and stir for a minute. Cover and let sit for an hour at desired temperature, check for total separation using a curd blade (or your finger). When the break is clean, cut the curds into 3/8" pieces and let them rest for 5 minutes. Gently mix the curds for 20 minutes. Give the curds five minutes to rest in the water bath.
3. 30% of the whey in the cooking pot should be drained. Replace the whey volume that was eliminated gradually with 160°F water and stir. The temperature ought to rise to 102°F as a result. Stirring the curds frequently will prevent them from tangling and also maintain the desired temperature about forty minutes.
4. After the curds have rested for five minutes at 102°F, slowly stir them for an additional 30 minutes. The final curds should be thoroughly cooked check to see if enough moisture has been drawn out. When pressed between the fingers, a broken curd should resist pressure only slightly. It should be firm throughout.
5. Remove the whey from the curds until it is about 2-3" above the settled curds, then let the curds settle to the bottom.
6. Using a medium-sized draining mat, carefully consolidate the curds to one side of the vat after draining the whey. Press firmly with your hands to form a tight mass as you consolidate the curds. Remove more whey if possible.
7. Fill a 2-pound cheesecloth-lined mold with the curds. Press the curds at 20 pounds for 30 minutes while covering them with one corner of the cheese cloth. Open the container, remove the cheese from the mold, and unwrap.
8. For thirty minutes, place the cheese in the warmed whey. Rewrap the cheese in cheese cloth after removing it from the whey bath, then put it back into the mold. For six hours, press at sixty pounds. Open the cheese cloth and remove the cheese from the press. The cheese is turned, wrapped once more in cheesecloth, and put through another six-hour press cycle at sixty pounds.
9. Take the cheese out of the press, then soak it for three hours in brine solution. Wax the cheese, place in your aging area and age it there for 4-6 weeks at 52-56°F and 80-85% moisture.

Cabra al Vino

Prep time:

Cook time:

Rest time:

Total time:

Yield: 2 pounds (900 g)

Ingredients:

- 2 gallons goat's milk
- 1/8 teaspoon MA4002 culture

- ¼ teaspoon calcium chloride diluted in ¼ cup cool, water
- ½ teaspoon fluid rennet, or ¼ tablet dry rennet, diluted in ¼ cup cool, water
- Red wine, enough to completely wash cheese, about 4 cups

Instruction:

1. Heat the milk to 95°F, slowly stir in the starter culture before covering. Give the milk ten minutes to age. If you're using homogenized milk, combine it with the diluted calcium chloride.
2. Add the diluted rennet, stir for a 5 minutes at 95°F. Cover and allow to sit for 1 ½ hours at the desired temperature,.
3. Make one cut with a curd blade to verify that there is a complete separation (or utilize your finger). Cut the curds into 1/2" pieces once you have a complete separation. Gently stir for 5 minutes and allow to rest for another 5 minutes in a water bath.
4. Remove 33% of the whey using a clean measuring cup. Add the hot water (175°F) little by little to replace the lost whey while stirring gradually to raise the curds' temperature to 100°F.
5. To prevent the curds from tangling constantly stir. When you reach the desired temperature, leave the curds to rest for ten minutes while continuing to stir them.
6. Using the cleaned measuring cup drain the whey till the level of the curds. Add the hot water and continue to mix until the curds reach a temperature of 100°F.
7. For 20 minutes, keep the desired temperature constant while stirring frequently to prevent the curds from tangling. Drain the whey after letting the curds sit in the pot for 30 minutes at 100°F.
8. Pour curds back into the pot and cut into 1/4" pieces. Add salt and stir.
9. Fill a 2-pound cheesecloth-lined mold with the curds. Press the curds at 20 pounds for 20 minutes while covering them with one corner of the cheese cloth.
10. Take the cheese out of the press, then gradually unwrap, turn the cheese over, wrap it again with the cloth, and press it for twelve hours at twenty pounds. Continue this cycle and press for a further twelve hours at 20 pounds.
11. Take the cheese out of the press. Unwrap it, add it to the brine solution, and let it sit there for two hours after 2 hours allow the cheese to surface dry. Wash it in a pot containing 4 cups of red wine for 24 hours. Remove the cheese, and let it air-dry for six hours, or until it is dry to the touch. Repeat the wine bath.
12. For at least three months, keep the cheese in your refrigerator at 50°F and 80–85 percent moisture. The cheese must be turned every day for the first 2 weeks. Apply brine solution to the cheese to clean it.

Red Leicester Cheese

Prep time: 5 minutes

Cook time: 60 minutes

Rest time: 2 hours

Total time: 3 hours 5 minutes

Yield: 2 pounds

Ingredients:

- 2 Gallons of Milk (Not Ultra Pasteurized)
- 1 teaspoon Annatto Cheese Coloring
- 1.5 Packets C101 Mesophilic or 3/8 tsp MA011 Culture
- ½ teaspoon Single Strength Liquid Rennet
- Salt
- Calcium Chloride (for pasteurized milk)

- 1/8 cup lard

Instructions:

1. Add annatto color to a half-cup of milk and stir until combined. Add the colored milk to the pot of milk.
2. Heat the milk to the desired temperature of 85°F and stir in the culture. For the next 60 minutes allow the milk to rest. Now carefully mix in the liquid rennet.
3. Until you have a clean break, leave the milk covered and at the desired temperature for 45 minutes while the culture develops and the rennet coagulates the curd (total separation). Cut the curds into 1/4 inch cubes once there is complete separation. Give the curds ten minutes to rest while maintaining the desired temperature.
4. The milk should gradually be heated for 45 minutes to a temperature of 95°F. The final curds should be thoroughly cooked before being checked to see if enough moisture has been drawn out. When pressed between the fingers, a broken curd should resist pressure only slightly. It should be firm throughout.
5. The curds can now be allowed to settle beneath the whey once this temperature is reached.
6. Drain the whey down to about 1 inch above the curd mass after the curds have been cooked and have briefly settled, stir gently about 15 minutes. The dry curds can now be poured into a butter muslin-lined colander.
7. The curd is ready to be drained after this brief rest, but it needs time to stay warm to continue turning lactose into lactic acid. The remaining whey should be drained, and the cheese should be tightly wrapped in cloth and pressed at a pressure of 15 pounds.
8. Cut the weight in half, then stack, rewrap, and press it after 30 minutes of rest (a warm environment can make this process easier). Repeat this process after 60 minutes, this will make the cheese more flatter and elongated.
9. After 60 minutes repeat the cut and stack process, allow the curds rest for 15 minutes. Break them into ¾ inch pieces and mix in salt
10. The curds can now be poured into a cheese mold that is lined with cheese cloth and put into a cheese press.
11. Start very light (20 pounds) when pressing and gradually increase the press weight to a moderate high level (150 pounds).
12. Using a light muslin that is cut to fit the shape of the cheese and applied with a thin layer of melted lard for adhesion, protect the cheese for aging. The cloth makes the surface much more breathable. Place the cheese back into the press after it has been completely covered, and press it for 12 hours at full weight.

13. The cloth ought to be embedded in the cheese surface when you remove it from the press. Any extra lard should now be on the surface and ready to be scraped off. If you follow these instructions, the finished cheese should have very little lard on it, and any leftover lard will be removed with the cloth.
14. The cheese is set for your aging space once it has been protected. Age the cheese at 52–56°F and 85–90% moisture for 6-9 months (or longer for stronger character).

Note: Since mold grows on the cloth only, it is not a problem. If it becomes too heavy, reduce the moisture, let it air dry a little, and give it one last brush to take some of it off.

Mozzarella

Prep Time: 1 hr 30 minutes

Cook Time: 20 minutes

Rest time: 1 hour

Total time: 1 hour 50 minutes

Ingredients:

- 1 gallon whole milk
- ½ teaspoons citric acid
- ½ cup water
- ¼ teaspoon liquid animal rennet
- 4 teaspoons salt

Instructions:

1. Combine Citric acid and ¼ cup water in a small bowl. Place aside. Mix in the rennet and the remaining ¼ cup water in a separate small bowl. Mix thoroughly, then set aside.
2. The milk and citric acid mixture should be combined and thoroughly mixed in a large pot over medium heat. Heat the milk to 90°F while stirring it frequently and with a thermometer about 5 minutes.
3. Stir in the rennet mixture after turning the heat off for a full 30 seconds. To ensure that the milk is thoroughly and evenly incorporated, stir the mixture from the bottom to the top. Place a lid on the pot and leave it alone for five minutes.
4. By slipping a knife between the milk and the pot's side, you can see if the curd has formed. Leave for another five minutes if necessary to rest.
5. Cut the curd into 1-inch-wide strips from top to bottom using a large knife. After that, make cuts in the other direction to create a grid pattern.
6. Bring the pot back to the burner and heat it slowly for about 5 minutes at 105°F. To ensure even heating, stir the liquid slowly while being careful not to disturb the curd.
7. Once more, turn off the heat and leave the pot alone for 10 minutes.
8. Prepare your colander for draining using a cheese cloth. Lift the curd from the pot with a slotted spoon, then set it down on the cheesecloth to drain. Use the cheesecloth as a squeeze aid while applying firm pressure to the curds to extract as much whey as you can.
9. The liquid (whey) in the pot is salted with 1 tablespoon of salt, remove four cups from the pot and warm the remaining whey.
10. Place the wrapped cheese for 10 seconds into the hot whey. Remove with a slotted spoon, and then, wearing gloves to protect your hands from the heat, stretch and fold the curd several times.
11. Return the curd (unwrapped) to the whey for an additional ten seconds, remove it, stretch the curd, and then add the 1 teaspoon of salt. When it has cooled, fold and stretch a few times before going back to the whey.
12. Repeat this procedure two or three times to transform the curds into shiny, silky, smooth mozzarella. When finished, form a smooth ball and tuck the edges under. This mozzarella ball should first be placed in the hot water to set its shape before being placed in the reserved cool whey to set for 15 minutes. Serve and enjoy.

Swiss Cheese

Prep time: 5 minutes

Cook time: 45 minutes

Rest time: 1 hour

Total time: 1 hour 50 minutes

Servings: 2 pounds

Ingredients:

- 2 Gallons of Milk
- 1/8 teaspoon MM100 Culture or 1 Pack C101 Mesophilic Culture
- 1/16 teaspoon Propionic Shermanii
- 1 teaspoon Single Strength Liquid Rennet
- Brine solution
- Calcium Chloride for Pasteurized Milk
- Liquid Rennet

Instructions:

1. Heat the milk to 84°F, add the starter culture gently and cover. Give the milk ten minutes to ripe. If you're using homogenized milk, add the diluted calcium chloride.
2. Include the diluted rennet and mix for one minute while maintaining the 90°F target temperature. For 60 minutes, cover and leave at the desired temperature. Slice through the curds to check for a complete separation using a curd blade (or your finger). Cut curds into 1/2" pieces once you have a clean break.
3. After five minutes of resting and gentle stirring, the curds should be set. Allow the curds to rest at the bottom of the vat for an additional five minutes after stirring.
4. Next, take out 1/3 of the whey with care this will lower the lactose so that the production of acid and bacteria will be slowed. The elastic texture of Baby Swiss is developed during this step.
5. In place of the whey, add hot water that is 130°F; in 10 minutes, the temperature of the curds will rise to 95°F; the curds will then be stirred slowly for 40 minutes. This will result in the desired dryness. Make sure to check the curds for the right amount of dryness: The final curds should be thoroughly cooked before being checked to see if enough moisture has been drawn out. When pressed between the fingers, a broken curd should resist pressure only slightly. It should be firm throughout.

6. Allow the curds to cool and solidify into a mass after they have finished cooking. To enhance better consolidation, try to gather them to one side of the pot.

7. Put a plate large enough to cover the curd mass on top of the curds after draining the whey to 1" above the cheese surface. Place a weight on top of the area equal to about 2 pounds, or about 1/2 of the expected curd weight. This will lessen any mechanical holes in the cheese body and help the warm curd nicely consolidate.

8. Remove the whey and transfer the curd mass into a mold lined with cloth. Press the cheese at 5 pounds for 2 hours. The cheese should be unwrapped, turned, then re-wrapped and pressed for five hours at 10 pounds.

9. The finished cheese ought to have a nice, tight rind without any gaps where molds could grow. As a result, cleaning and maintaining the surface will be much simpler as it ages. Right there, the cheese is set for its brine bath.

10. Place the cheese in a brine solution. Because the cheese will float, sprinkle 1 teaspoon of salt on top. After 2 hours, flip the cheese over and re-salt the surface (60 minutes).

11. The cheese should then be aged in a 65-70°F environment with 80% moisture for 3–4 weeks for larger holes or 2-3 weeks for smaller holes (this will be somewhat determined by the condition of your initial cool aging).

12. Make sure to turn the cheese every day to help distribute the moisture evenly, as this will affect the distribution and size of the holes. Maintain regular brushing for a natural rind.

13. For a month or longer to allow for flavor development, move to a cold room at 45–50°F and 85% moisture.

Blue Stilton

Prep time: 5 minutes

Cook time: 40 minutes

Rest time: 2 hours

Total time: 2 hours 45 minutes

Yield: 2 pounds

Ingredients:

- 2 gallons whole milk
- 2 cups light cream
- ¼ teaspoon Penicillium roqueforti
- 4 tablespoons mesophilic mother culture, or ¼ teaspoon mesophilic direct-set culture
- ¼ teaspoon fluid rennet or ¼ tablet dry rennet diluted in ¼ cup (60 ml) cool water
- 2 tablespoons cheese salt

Instructions:

1. Combine Cream and milk in a double boiler. Penicillium roqueforti should be added, then combine. When the milk mixture reaches 86°F, carefully stir in the starter culture before covering. Allow the milk to ripen at target temperature for 30 minutes, then stir in rennet.
2. The milk should be covered and allowed to sit at the desired temperature for 90 minutes. Examine the curds for total separation and slice them gently.
3. Place a colander in a sizable catch bowl and line it with cheese cloth. Pour the curds into the colander. The curds should rest in a whey pool once the process is finished.
4. In a hot water bath, let the mixture sit for one and a half hours at the desired temperature. Make a ball out of the cheese cloth by tying its edges together. To allow the whey to freely drain out of the curds, suspend a wooden spoon over a large pot and tie the closures around it. At room temperature, let the curds drain for thirty minutes.
5. Place the curd mixture on a cheese board while it is still in the cheese cloth once the whey has stopped draining. Put another cheese board on top of it and press it with a gallon container of water.
6. Clean two drying mats, a cheese board, a 2-pound cheese mold, and cheese cloth. Cut the curds into 1-inch pieces after removing them from the cheese cloth, sprinkle

salt. Use your fingers to delicately mix in the salt and curds in a bowl. Take care not to overwork the curds.

7. Line the cheese with cheese cloth, and place it on top of one of the drying mats. Place the mat on top of the cheese board. Then gently pour the curds into the mold, cover it with another cheese mat. Turn the cheese by setting your hands on both the top and base of the cheese mat and flipping it over. Do this 2 times per hour.

8. For the next four days, while keeping the cheese in the mold, turn it four times each day. (Since the cheese has not been pressed, the molds will help it maintain its shape.) Clean your punching tool, then poke twenty holes through the cheese's top and base.

9. Place the cheese in your aging box at 55°F with 90% dampness, let it sit on the cheese mat, cover it, and then store it. Three times per week, turn the cheese, and once per week, clear it off by wiping it down with a cloth dipped in brine solution. Age the cheese for four months at 55 °F and 85% humidity.

Parmesan

Prep time: 10 minutes

Cook time: 45 minutes

Rest time: 2 hours

Total time: 2 hours 55 minutes

Yield: 2 pounds

Ingredients

- 2 gallons low-fat milk
- 8 tablespoons (60 ml) thermophilic mother culture, or ¼ teaspoon (around 2 ml) thermophilic direct-set culture
- 1 teaspoon (5 ml) fluid rennet, or ¼ tablet dry rennet, diluted in ¼ cup (60 ml) cool, unchlorinated water
- Brine solution

Instruction:

1. Heat the milk to 92°F, stir in the starter culture into the milk. Mature the milk while covered for 30 minutes. Maintaining a constant 92°F objective temperature, add the diluted rennet and stir for two minutes.

2. For forty minutes, or until there is complete separation, cover and leave the mixture at the desired temperature. Check by cutting a piece of curd with a knife or your finger. Once the curds have completely separated, cut them into 1/4 inch blocks and stir them slowly for 10 minutes. The milk should gradually reach 100°F after 25 minutes.

3. Use your whisk consistently to combine. The cooking pot should be taken out of the double boiler and placed on the burner. Bring the temperature up to 130°F gradually. This should only take a few minutes, and There will be some grain size in the curds. In order to prevent curd loss, let the curds rest for five minutes, cover the pot with a plate, and drain off the whey.

4. Fill a 2-pound cheesecloth-lined mold with the curds. Place a follower on top, cover one corner of the curds with cheese cloth, and press at five pounds for fifteen minutes. Remove the cheese from the press, then gradually start to unwrap.

5. Turn the cheese over, cover it once more with the cloth, and press it for 30 minutes at 10 pounds. Follow this procedure again, pressing for two hours at fifteen pounds. Repeat for twelve hours while applying 20 pounds of pressure.

6. Open the cheese cloth and remove the cheese from the mold. Put the cheese in the brine solution, ensure to flip the cheese occasionally for 24 hours at 70°F.

7. The cheese should be taken out of the brine, cleaned off, and placed on a cheese board. For at least three months, place the cheese in the refrigerator at 55°F and 80–85% humidity. For the first month, turn the cheese every day. After that, turn it once in a week.

8. The brine should be used to clean off any mold that develops on the cheese's exterior. After two months, rub the cheese with olive oil to prevent drying out. Over the course of aging for six months to two years, wipe the cheese with olive oil a few times.

Romano

Prep time: 10 minutes

Cook time: 45 minutes

Rest time: 2 hours

Total time: 2 hours 55 minutes

Yield: 2 pounds

Ingredients

- 2 gallons milk (1 gallon whole and 1 gallon low fat)
- 8 tablespoons thermophilic mother culture, or ¼ teaspoon direct-set culture
- ¼ teaspoon lipase powder dissolved in ¼ cup cool water
- ¾ teaspoon of fluid rennet or ¼ tablet dried rennet weakened in ¼ cup cool, unchlorinated water
- Lipase (optional)
- Brine solution

Procedures:

1. In a container with 8 tablespoons of milk sprinkle lipase on the surface to rehydrate before stirring about 20 minutes.
2. Heat the remaining milk to 90°F, stir in the starter culture and add milk-lipase mixture, cover and permit the milk to mature for an hour at 90°F.
3. Add the rennet and stir for at least 2 minutes, cover and let it rest for 40 minutes, or until there is complete separation, cover it and leave it at the desired temperature. Cut into 1/4 inch. Give the curds ten minutes to rest while maintaining the desired temperature.
4. Heat the milk gradually until it reaches 115°F; this should take 45 minutes. Frequently use the whisk to stir. Once you reach the desired temperature, continue cooking for an additional 45 minutes while mixing frequently to prevent the curds from tangling.
5. Through a cheesecloth-lined colander positioned over a catch bowl, drain the whey. Fill a 2-pound cheesecloth-lined mold with the curds. Press the curds at ten pounds for thirty minutes while covering one corner with cheese cloth.
6. Take the cheese out of the press, then gradually start to unwrap. Turn the cheese over, cover it once more with the cloth, and press it for three hours at 25 pounds.

Use this system again, pressing for 12 hours at 40 pounds. Press twelve more times at twenty pounds.

7. Open the cheese cloth and remove the cheese from the mold. Place the cheese in the brine solution. The cheese should be turned occasionally and left undisturbed in the salt water at 70°F for 24 hours.

8. Cheese should be taken out of the brine, cleaned off, and put on a cheese board. Start by turning the cheese every day for the first three month of ripening, then week by week after that. Refrigerate the cheese for ten months at 55°F and 80-85% humidity.

9. Brush the cheese with brine solution to get rid of any mold that develops on the outside. Rub some olive oil on the cheese after a month to prevent drying out, and again after seven days. Repeat every month.

Neufchâtel

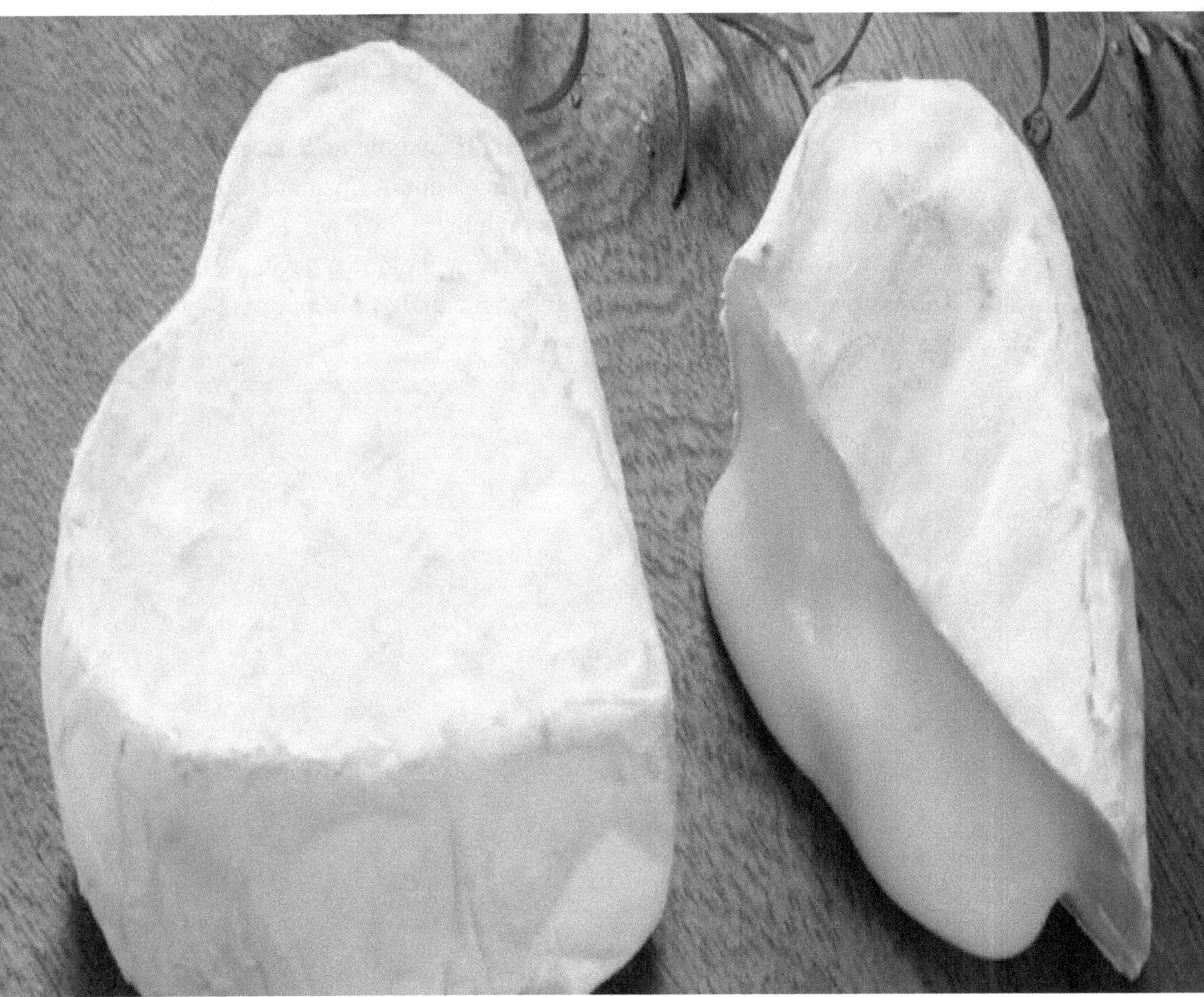

Prep time: 5 minutes

Cook time: 5 minutes

Rest time: 20 hours

Total time: 20 hours 10 minutes

Yield: 1 pounds

Ingredients:

- 1 gallon (4L) whole milk
- 16 tablespoons (240 ml) prepared mesophilic mother culture, or ¼ teaspoon (around 2 ml) mesophilic direct-set culture
- 3 drops fluid rennet dissolved in ⅓ cup (90 ml) cool water
- ¼ teaspoon Penicillium candidum

Procedures:

1. Heat milk to 80°F, stir in penicillium candidum and the starter culture. Add 1 teaspoon of the rennet and gently stir. Cover the milk and allow it to rest for 20 hours at target temperature.
2. Scoop the curds into a colander lined with cheesecloth once they have a firm surface. Tie the cheesecloth into a ball, fold the closures over a spoon, and hang it to drain for eight to twelve hours. Before pressing, the cheese needs to have a firm texture and wrap up its whey.
3. Place the curd cloth into the colander once more and spread it out using a plate and catch bowl below.
4. Use a light weight to press (1 pound). Set aside in your refrigerator for twelve hours to drain.
5. Remove the curds from the cheesecloth and pour them into the desired molds. Place in a ripening box at 45°F and 90% stickiness when the fruit is firm. Allow the cheese to mature for seven to ten days, at which point the cheese should have a layer of white mold on it.
6. Cheese should be taken out of the ripening box and covered with wax paper or cheese film. Continue aging for a further three weeks, or until the cheese is soft to the touch in the center. This cheese can be stored for at least a month.

Gruyère

Prep time: 5 minutes

Cook time: 10 minutes

Rest time: 1 hour

Total time:

Yield: 2 pounds

Ingredients:

- 2 gallons (8 L) whole milk
- 2 tablespoons thermophilic mother culture, or ¼ teaspoon thermophilic direct-set culture
- 1 teaspoon propionic shermanii powder dissolved in ¼ cup milk
- ½ teaspoon fluid rennet
- Brine solution

Instructions:

1. Mix the starter culture into the milk after it has warmed to 90°F. Add the milk and the dissolved propionic shermanii, and combine thoroughly. At 90°F, cover the milk and allow it to age for ten minutes.
2. Include the diluted rennet and mix for one minute while maintaining an objective temperature of 90° F. At the highest temperature, cover it and let it sit for 40 minutes, or until there is complete separation.
3. Cut the curds into 1"shaped pieces when the separation is complete. Mix the curds for 40 minutes while maintaining the 90°F objective temperature. To achieve a consistent curd shape, use a wire balloon whisk.
4. Bring the temperature up to 120°F gradually. About 35 minutes should pass during this. To prevent the curds from tangling, stir frequently. Once the desired temperature has been reached, maintain it for 30 minutes and continue mixing with a whisk.
5. At 120°F, let the curds rest for five minutes. Fill a 2-pound cheesecloth-lined mold with the curds. Press the curds at ten pounds for fifteen minutes, covering one corner of the curds with cheese cloth, top with follower.
6. Remove the cheese from the press, then gradually start to unwrap. After flipping the cheese over, rewrap it in cheese cloth, and press it for 30 minutes at 15 pounds.

Repeat this strategy, pressing for six hours at thirty pounds. Press once more for fifty pounds.

7. Place the cheese in the brine after removing it from the press. After allowing the cheese soak in the brine for twelve hours, occasionally flip it. Put the cheese on the cheese board after removing it from the brine solution and wiping it clean. Your refrigerator should be set to 55°F and 85% humidity for the cheese.
8. For the first fourteen days, make sure to turn the cheese every day, and then once a week for up to two months. Place the cheese in the refrigerator to mature for at least eight months.

Camembert Cheese

Prep time: 5 minutes

Cook time: 5 minutes

Rest time: 2 hours

Total time: 2 hours 10 minutes

Ingredients:

- 1 gallon fresh whole milk
- 2 cups cream
- ¼ teaspoon Flora Danica or Mesophilic Type B cheese culture

- 1/8 teaspoon Penicillium camemberti mold culture
- 1/32 taspoon Geotrichum Candidum
- 1/8 teaspoon rennet
- 3 teaspoons fine sea salt

Directions:

1. Heat the milk to a temperature of 85°F, combine it with the starter culture and Penicillium candidum. For one and a half hours, keep the cover on while the milk matures.
2. Include the diluted rennet and stir for two minutes while maintaining the desired temperature of 85°F. For an hour, or until there is complete separation, cover and leave the mixture at the desired temperature.
3. Slice one of the curds with a curd blade to check for total separation. Put the cheese mold and mats in boiling water to sanitize them while hoping that the curds will set. When the curds have completely separated, cut them into 1/2-inch cubes and gently stir for 15 minutes while maintaining the desired temperature.
4. Once the curds have cooled to the desired temperature for an additional 15 minutes, drain off the whey using a clean measuring cup to the same level as the curds. It will have the appearance of watery cottage cheese.
5. Place two cheese cloth-lined molds on one of the cheese mats that you have placed on top of your drain pan. Scoop the curds into the molds with care, working your way to the top. Put a cheese mat over the molds once they are full. At room temperature, allow the cheese to drain for an hour. As the whey is drained from the cheese through the sides and base, you will witness an amazing fall in the cheese level.
6. Flip the cheeses (place one hand underneath, and another hand on top of the upper mat. Holding the top and base firmly, lift them up, and in one fast movement, flip them over and set them back on head of the draining dish. Check to see that the mold isn't sticking by gently peeling back the mat, making sure that it doesn't tear the edges of the cheese). Flip your cheeses, 12 times in 12 hours, until they have pulled away from the sides of the molds completely.
7. Pull the cheese's mold with care. If the cheese sticks to the mold, slide a thin blade in between them to aid in the process.
8. Salt the cheeses lightly and set them aside on a cheese board to rest for ten minutes at room temperature.
9. Put the cheeses on one of the mats, place them in your ripening box, and refrigerate them at 45°F and 85% humidity. After five days, a thin film of mold should start to

appear on the surface. The cheese should be turned over, put back in the ripening box, and placed inside the 45°F refrigerator. Continue to ripen for an additional 10 days. The cheese should now have a sizable layer of mold covering its surface.

10. Cheese should be taken out of the ripening box and covered in cheese film. Give the cheese a month to mature at 45 °F.

Asiago

Prep time: 10 minutes

Cook time: 30 minutes

Rest time: 2 hour

Total time: 2 hours 40 minutes

Ingredients:

- 1½ gallon whole milk
- ½ gallon skim milk
- ½ teaspoon direct-set thermophilic culture
- ½ teaspoon fluid rennet diluted in ¼ cup cool water
- Brine solution

Instructions:

1. In a sizable pot over low heat, mix the milk. For 30 minutes, raise the temperature gradually to 92°F.
2. Sprinkle the starter over the milk's surface and mix it in. After allowing it to rehydrate for about five minutes, mix it in thoroughly for 60 minutes.
3. For 45 minutes, keep the milk covered and the temperature at 92°F. Stir in the rennet after this aging period, cover it, and let it sit at 92°F for 60 minutes to set.
4. Cut the curd into pieces measuring 1/2 inches in length and allow them to rest for about five minutes after the curd has completely separated. Start gradually raising the temperature until it reaches 104°F. Remove the curds from the heat once they reach 104°F, then stir them slowly for 15 minutes.
5. Put the pot back on the stove at a low heat and gradually raise the temperature until it reaches 118°F while continuously mixing. When the curds reach this temperature, stop stirring them and let them settle. Keep the temperature at 118°F by covering.
6. Use a spoon to scoop out the whey until the highest points of the curds are all that remain. putting a cheesecloth-lined colander over a bowl for draining. Fill the prepared molds with the warm cheese curds. Overlap the curds with the cheesecloth. Then using your hand, gently press the curds into the mold.
7. Place a follower on top of the filled mold and press for 60 minutes at 8 pounds of weight.

8. Remove, rotate, and rewrap the cheese before pressing at 8 pounds once more for an additional 8 hours.

9. Make about a gallon of brine solution and warm it to 50°F while the cheese is being pressed. Remove the curd from the molds after it has been pressed, then submerge it in the brine. For 12 hours, keep them in a cool location, like the refrigerator. During this time, turn a couple of times.

10. The cheeses should be taken out of the brine solution and cleaned. Place them on a drying rack, then cover with a fresh piece of cheesecloth. Let the cheese air-dry for a few days or until the outside feels completely dry. Throughout the drying process, turn the cheese a few times.

11. The cheeses should be placed in an aging box and covered. Maintain a cool, moist environment (Optimal humidity is 85%.) For three weeks, brush the cheeses with a salt solution about twice a week to prevent mold and promote rind development. The Asiago will be ready to serve after three weeks, but you can age it for up to a year by only brushing it twice a week.

Limburger

Prep time: 10 minutes

Cook time: 30 minutes

Rest time: 2 hours

Total time: 2hours 40 minutes

Yield: 2

Ingredients

- 2 Gallons Whole Milk
- 1 Packet C21 Buttermilk Culture or ¼ teaspoon MM100 Culture
- 1/16 teaspoon C70 Geotrichum Candidum
- 1/16 teaspoon C10 Bacteria Linens
- ½ teaspoon Single Strength Liquid Rennet
- ½ teaspoon Annatto coloring (optional)
- ½ teaspoon Calcium Chloride (for pasteurized milk)

Procedure:

1. To 90°F, warm the milk. Then stir in the culture, 1/32 teaspoon Geotrichum Candidum, and 1/32 teaspoon Bacteria Linens after letting them sit without being disturbed for two minutes. If necessary, incorporate calcium chloride and annatto color. The milk needs 30 minutes of 90°F ripening.
2. When the milk is fully matured, add the diluted rennet and let the milk sit for an hour to set.
3. It's time to cut the curds and release the whey once a firm curd has been formed (if it's still too delicate, let it rest for an additional 15 minutes). The curd size should be between 1/2 and 5/8 inches, and the cutting should be gradual.
4. Allow the curds to settle with whey on top after gently stirring it for 20 minutes. For 10 minutes, gradually heat the curds to the desired temperature. Scoop off the whey, leaving the curd mass and a thin layer of whey at the bottom of the container.
5. Place the cleaned molds on draining mats and transfer the curds along with the remaining whey. Following the transfer of all the curd to the molds, a second draining mat should be placed on top, and the mold should be rotated with the mats to drain the whey and keep the curd mass contained. Make sure to rotate the curd at

least four times in 60 minutes, and then periodically over the following hours (6 hours).

6. Salt the cheese by placing it in a brine solution for two hours (the cheese will be above the brine surface; sprinkle salt on it; let it sit for two minutes; then flip it over and sprinkle salt again; after salting, wipe the surface; do not let it dry; this is because moisture is required for curing).

7. Then, put the curds in a plastic container to maintain a high moisture level and initially a temperature of 58–62°F. Put a cheese mat under the cheese and make sure to turn it every day for five days, wash the cheese in a light salt solution using a cloth or brush.

8. If you prefer a milder cheese, wash off the top layer; however, if you prefer a cheese with strong aroma and flavor, wash only lightly. To promote uniform ripening, wash the cheese three times over the course of nine days at 45°F.

9. Cure the cheese for a minimum of 7 months. While younger cheese is crumbly and sweet, older cheese is bitter and has a strong flavor.

Muenster

Prep time: 5 minutes

Cook time: 20 minutes

Rest time: 2 hours

Total time: 2 hours 25 minutes

Yield: 2 pounds

Ingredients:

- 2 gallons whole milk
- ¼ teaspoon mesophilic direct-set culture
- ½ teaspoon fluid rennet
- Brine solution
- ½ teaspoon B. linens diluted in cool water

Procedures

1. Mix the starter culture into the milk after it has warmed to 90°F. After blending, wait 15 minutes at the target temperature. Add the rennet, then blend for two minutes.
2. For forty minutes, or until you obtain a complete separation, cover the milk and allow it to rest at the desired temperature.
3. To check for a clean break, insert a curd blade and cut through the curds once. When the curds have completely separated, cut them into 3/8" pieces and allow them to rest for five minutes at the target temperature.
4. For more than 30 minutes, gradually raise the curd temperature to 100°F, while mixing to prevent the curds from tangling. For an additional 30 minutes, maintain the desired temperature of 100°F while mixing once more to prevent the curds from tangling.
5. Allow the curds to rest at the desired temperature for five minutes. Using a clean measuring cup, drain the whey until it is the same consistency as the curds. Place the camembert molds on top of cheese mats after scooping the curds into clean, camembert molds. After allowing the curds to drain for 30 minutes at room temperature, turn the molds and mat into a sizable catch bowl.
6. Repeat this cycle at regular intervals for five times, allow the cheese to rest for 12 hours at room temperature on a cheese drying mat. Eliminate the cheese from the

molds, and put it in the salt water solution in the fridge for twelve hours at 50°F. Ensure to flip the cheese in the salt water to guarantee a nice covering.

7. Remove the cheese from the brine after twelve hours, then pat dry with a towel. Put the hydrated B. linens in a spray can, and softly spray the cheeses. Put the cheese in the ripening box and keep it there for two weeks at 60 degrees and 95% humidity.

8. Every day, clean the cheeses with a cloth dipped in a salt water solution. This will facilitate the consistent distribution of B. materials throughout the cheese. After 14 days, remove the cheese from the aging box and let it air dry in the refrigerator at 50°F and 95% humidity.

9. Age for 6 weeks, turning every day. Each third day, wipe the cheese down with a damped cloth in brine

Butter

Prep time: 15 minutes

Servings: ¾ pound butter

Ingredients:

- 2 ½ cups heavy cream
- 1 cup sour cream
- 1 teaspoon coarse sea salt
- Freshly ground black pepper

Directions:

1. A medium-sized bowl of ice water should be ready. Whip the cream and sour cream gradually in the bowl of an electric stand mixer with the whisk attachment. As the

cream begins to separate and the mixture begins to thicken, increase the mixer's speed and continue whipping.

2. The butter should be gathered up with a rubber spatula and taken out of the bowl. There will naturally be some liquid as a byproduct of this process. Actually, that liquid is buttermilk.

3. Gather the ball of butter together into a double layer of cheesecloth and put it into the ice bath to wash any buttermilk off the surface. Sprinkle with salt and pepper, to taste. Pack the butter into a bowl or roll it into a ball or log shape using plastic wrap, your butter is set.

Ghee

Prep time: 5 minutes

Cook time: 30 minutes

Total time: 35 minutes

Servings: 3

Ingredients

1 pound organic, unsalted butter

Instructions:

1. Cut the butter into cubes and place in a small pot.
2. Gently heat the sliced butter till it melt and start foaming, skim off the top foam continuously as you keep heating
3. Continue cooking the ghee on low for another 20-25 minutes, or until the middle layer is translucent and the smell is fragrant. At this point you should see some milk solids at the bottom of the pan.
4. Turn off the heat and let the ghee cool for a few minutes. Then strain the ghee through cheesecloth into a glass container, your ghee is ready. Enjoy

Nutrition

Calories: 124kcal

Fat: 14g	Fat 8g	Cholesterol 36mg